THE OTHER SIDE OF THE ICE

One Family's Treacherous Journey Negotiating
the Northwest Passage

SPRAGUE THEOBALD

WITH

Allan Kreda

D1166073

SKYHORSE PUBLISHING

Dedication

To the officers and crews of HMS Erebus *and HMS* Terror—*men whose lives and courage were not in vain, and whose spirits stand eternal watch over a hallowed and fragile land.*

Skyhorse Publishing books may be purchased in bulk at special discounts for sales promotion, corporate gifts, fund-raising, or educational purposes. Special editions can also be created to specifications. For details, contact the Special Sales Department, Skyhorse Publishing, 307 West 36th Street, 11th Floor, New York, NY 10018 or info@skyhorsepublishing.com.

Skyhorse® and Skyhorse Publishing® are registered trademarks of Skyhorse Publishing, Inc.®, a Delaware corporation.

Visit our website at www.skyhorsepublishing.com.

10 9 8 7 6 5 4 3 2 1

Library of Congress Cataloging-in-Publication Data is available on file.

Cover design by Brian Peterson

Print ISBN: 978-1-63450-298-6

Printed in the United States of America

PHOTO CREDITS: Front cover photograph—Greg DeAscentis

All photographs property of Hole In The Wall Productions and contributed by Sprague Theobald, Chauncey Tanton, Dominique Tanton, Sefton Theobald, Greg DeAscentis, and Clinton Bolton.

CONTENTS

ACKNOWLEDGMENTS

From first conception of the trip, to final edit of the book, many wonderfully supportive people have given their time and efforts to the cause; some stayed on for the duration of the journey, while others were only able to give what time they had and helped from afar. Regardless the time committed, all ensured that the project came to a successful conclusion, a conclusion far greater than my original dream allowed. So, below and in no specific order, I extend my deepest, most heartfelt thanks and appreciation to . . .

. . . Dan and Marcia Streech for their unwavering support and fervent belief that this journey could be accomplished. Adaline for never allowing me to give up. Matt Dutra of Rubic Design for helping to get the word out. E'Loise Toppa Tamer for being our No. 1 Fan. Michelle Marden, Tony Linder, and Julie Moreau Reichling, who all helped in their own unique way. Helly Hansen and Oakley for helping us with gear. Allan Kreda for the original article on the trip and his ensuing enthusiasm and drive. My agent Doug Grad for believing in me and the story. Tony Lyons at Skyhorse Publishing for taking the chance and letting me share the adventure. Jay Cassell, Editorial Director at Skyhorse, for his unflagging patience in listening to my gripes and stepping in to get the book moving in a proper and true direction. The gang on Squirrel Island for allowing me quiet time to write. My editor, Tom McCarthy, for being a great human, a brilliant editor, and for making me look far better than I actually am.

There are many, many others who helped immeasurably, unfortunately far too many to list here. I hope that you all know who you are and please know that you too have my deepest and most sincere thanks for helping bring this dream to fruition.

—*Sprague*

PROLOGUE

Before grabbing a book and heading below, I took a stroll out on deck to try to gather in the towering strength and beauty of the mountains that surrounded our still and peaceful anchorage, perhaps the most stunning I'd ever seen. Low, shrub-covered flats quickly ran up to rocky foothills that rose straight up into the monstrous snow-covered peaks. It was an area waiting to be hiked and explored but, for me at least, only after a good night's sleep. Sometime during the past day, we had crossed an invisible line that moved everyday thinking to a seldom-visited level.

We were anchored now in an area much more raw, powerful, and potentially threatening than we had experienced. On our way into this amazing paradise, we encountered, for the first time, charts that simply didn't have complete soundings, no channel markers, no warning of shoals or hidden rock outcroppings. While we weren't exactly flying blind, we were navigating in an area of greatly reduced information. Not for the first time in the trip the thought struck, "If we stick here, we are screwed."

This new level of thinking and awareness was debilitating, a slowly circling feeling of expected isolation and self-reliance. No longer would a potential emergency be met with a simple call on the ship's radio to the local Coast Guard or towboat. We were becoming increasingly isolated and as such were going to have to rely on our own wits. My hope was that this mounting sense of isolation would stay beyond the limits of the boat and not work its way inside. Time would tell. For the past two years, the talk had been to simply get to this area and then farther north.

I unexpectedly found my senses coming alive. My sense of smell was more acute, my hearing was finer, and my sight was more focused. It was a feeling, a new way of seeing life, that through the rest of the trip would reach far deeper than I could have imagined.

The Northwest Passage is a ship killer, and always has been.

At various stages of the journey, I found myself numb. Exhausted. Terrified.

How had it all started? What were we doing?

I was leading a crossing of the Northwest Passage, an 1,800-mile channel north of the Arctic Circle, connecting, in theory, the Atlantic and Pacific Oceans. Hundreds of sailors had given their lives trying to do the exact same thing. We were a small boat with a small crew. *Bagan* is a fifty-seven foot long Nordhavn, and she was manned by six of us, three of whom were my children.

As a filmmaker, I hoped to document our passage. As a parent, I had a chance to try to readjust the past. Since a divorce more than fifteen years earlier, my children and I hadn't had the luxury of living together, and this trip was the first time the four of us were under the same roof for any length of time.

One thought and one thought only kept shouting in my mind, a thought that no expedition leader and, especially, no parent should ever have to think; a thought that held me in a cold, mental death grip, a thought that I still think about.

"Have I brought us all together just to lead us to our deaths?"

CHAPTER 1

THE HISTORY OF A DREAM

It was a quintessential summer day in 1957 on Squirrel Island, three miles off Maine's Boothbay Harbor, about an hour north of Portland. I was six years old and eagerly settling myself into the twelve-foot sailboat that was securely tied to a floating dock in the island's cove.

Once in, I briefly turned my back to the dock to take stock of this small yet fascinating wooden boat. I pressed myself up into the bow to make room for my mother, who was taking me out for my introduction to the world of sailing. Suddenly, with a forward jerk, the boat took on a life of its own and silently glided out into the calm cove, without my mother in it. I quickly looked at the retreating dock and shouted to my mother, who purposely had stayed on land, "What do I do?"

My mother took a drag on her ever-present Viceroy. She grinned and, with her typical New England pragmatism, offered back, "You'll figure it out!" Thus began my first sailing lesson.

The boat had one sail and one very obvious tiller slowly flopping back and forth. Surely that had something to do with steering. The sail seemed to be adjusted with a small rope, and it appeared that if the sail were just so, it would capture the wind and help to move the small boat along.

Through trial and error, I did manage to "figure it out." I sailed the 100 yards across the small cove, gently bumped against the rocks, hopped out into the freezing Maine water no more than two feet deep to get her turned around, climbed back in, and sailed back across the cove, hitting the dock with great ceremony as I landed.

I was exhilarated, ecstatic, enamored. And I was beyond pissed off at my mother for pulling her trick. Looking back, I can clearly see that this woman, an accomplished sailor in her own right, did what she felt best. Perhaps it was an unorthodox and extreme lesson, but our mutual smiles of delight became cemented into my memory one very special gleaming summer day all those years ago.

That was my start of a very long, loving, challenging, and sometimes dysfunctional relationship with boats and the sea.

I'd been aware that for centuries, hundreds of men had died trying to find the secret to the Northwest Passage, an 1,800-mile Arctic route between the Atlantic and Pacific oceans. I'd read about the Franklin Expedition of the 1840s, when 129 men sailing two ice-tested, state-of-the-art 120-foot ships— *Erebus* and *Terror,* the equivalents of seagoing Sherman tanks—simply vanished. The little we know about what happened to those courageous nineteenth-century explorers consists of lead poisoning from the improperly canned food, ships broken by the ice, starvation, and cannibalism. Not a pretty picture. I also knew that it wasn't until 1906 that Roald Amundsen became the first to accomplish the feat—and it took him parts of three years.

Since Amundsen's successful transit, perhaps twenty-four pleasure boats had made a successful crossing. Various commercial attempts have occasionally been made. In 1969, the oil tanker *SS Manhattan* did manage a crossing. At one point, the tanker became hopelessly stuck, requiring aid from the Canadian icebreakers CCGS *John A. Macdonald* and the CCGS *Louis S. St-Laurent.* During the rescue, the *Macdonald* broke her starboard propeller in heavy ice, an inglorious start for future shipping concerns. A later winter attempt to cross The Passage proved impossible. Since 1969, shipping there has been local—isolated community to isolated community.

Attempts by pleasure boats over the years—smaller, private sailboats and trawlers not specifically designed with double-steel hulls or for ice encounters—have been rare. And the few who made it successfully usually needed two to three seasons, usually a small, two- to three-week window either side of the end of July.

Crossing this "Arctic Grail" had always been lodged in the deep recesses of my nautical thinking, but never articulated any more than my wish to walk on the moon or dive the deepest ocean depths. My quest never possessed an actual voice—or so I thought until a 2007 dinner at a fine Madison Avenue restaurant in New York City.

I was invited to dinner by a friend and was at a table with four others, three of whom I didn't know. I'm not very good in situations like that and tend to listen rather than talk. But I must have talked enough because at one point I heard the question, "So, with all your sea miles, what would be your dream trip, the ultimate expedition?"

Mouth working far faster than brain, I immediately came back with, "To do the Northwest Passage," a conversation stopper if ever there was one. I went on to tell how I felt it was perhaps the last great boating adventure. Hundreds of men died or simply vanished trying, existing charts were nineteenth century at best, and there was no guarantee one would make it to the other side alive. If polar bears didn't get you, the ice could. Plus, I added, as a filmmaker, it would be the opportunity of a lifetime.

I went on to say how I'd watched with frustration as the television networks and the media in general reported on global warming for the last few years, yet no one had sent a camera team up and into Canada's historic Northwest Passage to talk to the people who live there.

The ensuing silence at the table was deafening. What was ironic was that the others had met aboard an adventure cruise ship to the Antarctic a year earlier, the other end of the world but an area that offered up the same killer ice and violent storms. They were enthralled to hear what I had to say. It got me pretty excited, too.

It clearly was an idea whose time had come.

One of my self-regulating tests of whether an idea is good is how I feel about it the next morning. When I was younger, these brainstorms were usually filed under the category "seemed like a good idea at the time." They were late-night epiphanies usually fueled by vast amounts of alcohol, so much so that when I was twenty-seven, booze and I had a parting of the ways; it was destroying what hopes and joys I had in life. After waking up for the umpteenth time on a vomit-stained mattress in an otherwise bare apartment, I decided it was time to face the facts. Growing up in a single parent and abusively alcoholic household, coupled with suffering drastically with dyslexia during my school days at an indifferent school that regarded me as "stupid," I found comfort and escape in self-medication.

To this day, I'm amazed that I didn't end up in jail.

Getting sober at twenty-seven took a brutal self-examination and strong desire to get painfully honest with myself. Unbeknownst to me, my then thirty-year commitment to sobriety was going to come into play on the trip. Since I stopped drinking, life has been more predictable, but thankfully not too predictable.

After shooting off my mouth at dinner, I awoke the next morning with an overwhelming sense of purpose. I started sending emails letting friends and associates know of my thoughts to transit the Northwest Passage in the summer of 2009.

It wasn't as crazy a decision as it sounded. I had been sailing since I was six. I had delivered numerous boats from New England to the Virgin Islands and back. I had crewed on the twelve-meter America's Cup racer *Intrepid*, raced "big boats," participated in the Two Man Transatlantic Race, and taken my own boat to Bermuda and beyond many times.

When I was racing sailboats, my area of specialty was the foredeck; as physically a challenging spot on a boat as any. I found that lugging around 100-plus-pound wet sails on a bouncing foredeck in the dark of night was about as happy a place as I could be. My back, however, did not share in my joy.

After two ruptured disks (the second of which temporarily paralyzed my left leg—a leg that to this day has very little feeling) and the resultant back surgeries, I moved from sailboats to powerboats, specifically trawlers—and began my long history with Nordhavn Yachts.

I took my first Nordhavn 46 from California to Alaska where I cruised the Inside Passage for months. Several years later, I moved up to a Nordhavn 57 and brought her from California to Rhode Island through the Panama Canal. Whether it was maxi-sailboats, America's Cup twelve-meters, private yachts, or my own sailboats and trawlers, from the start of my professional sailing in the 1970s until just before the Northwest Passage trip, I had amassed about 40,000 offshore miles. My boat at the time of the decision to do The Passage was a Nordhavn 57, *Bagan*—a perfect long-distance cruiser that could comfortably hold a crew of six.

One of the many emails that I sent was to my good friend Dan Streech, president of Nordhavn Yachts in Dana Point, California. Within hours, Dan called me and said, "I'm in, how can I help?" I'd first met Dan in 1992 when I fell in love with one of Nordhavn's designs, their flagship "46," which I planned to use as a floating production facility. I scraped together what funding I could find and approached Nordhavn, and our friendship flourished.

During the early 1990s, when Nordhavn was trying to establish its name, they were hit by the Gulf War-induced recession. Together, Dan and I weathered this financial storm. His costs to build the boat were constantly fluctuating, and my ability to secure a loan to purchase the boat was stretched. In the end, I came out with an amazing boat and a friend for life.

Two days after receiving Dan's encouraging news on the Northwest Passage trip, I was in Dana Point at a conference table with Dan and his partner Jim Leishman, recounting the remarkable and tragic history of man's attempt to cross this 1,800-mile northern route between Atlantic and Pacific, a route sought despite its dangers because it would shave thousands of miles off the traditional routes of going around The Horn or through the Panama Canal.

I told them that win, lose, or sink, I wanted to try to add to my list of awards for my filmwork—which included an Emmy in 1982 for my documentary on the America's Cup—and make a documentary about The Passage, with my journey as the centerpiece. I told them that the plan, if it was to work, was to leave from Newport, Rhode Island, and get up to Greenland after short stays in Halifax and Newfoundland. From Greenland, wait for the ice in The Passage to open, hopefully get through in one piece, and once out, head for Seattle with stops in Barrow, Nome, and Sitka, Alaska. Then head down through British Columbia's Inside Passage.

I had no money, but I did have a projected $400,000 budget. They were a step or two ahead of me and offered a sponsorship backing of $300,000. They were thinking of having a forty-foot boat built and beefed up to tag along with me to try the trip in tandem. Jim hoped that Nordhavn could gain some great publicity, adding to that garnered when one of their forty-foot models circumnavigated the world—unheard of for a trawler that size. We agreed it would be smart to try and get up to The Passage on an ice breaker a year before I was to attempt it to see the conditions we would encounter on our trip.

The deal was struck with a handshake, something that has always been a double-edged sword for me. I was assured paperwork would follow. One of my many faults is that I trust people and expect that apart from extremely adverse situations, they will do as they say they will. Naïve? Perhaps, but it's a philosophy that has kept me at great peace with myself.

I headed home with a new sense of conviction and purpose, announcing my decision in a flurry of emails to friends. Now I would need to create a website, find people to help raise funds, and find a screenwriter, potential director, and someone to help with publicity. Few people in the media knew what the Northwest Passage was or why my attempting a transit with a film crew was so important. I had to round up a crew of people who were willing to give up to six months of their lives for little or no pay.

I especially needed a project manager, and someone to help set up and run the "domestic" side of the actual trip, which was crucial, and perhaps the most expensive. The domestic side included the feeding and caring of the crew, which would number about six. Enter my stepdaughter, Dominique Tanton, and her boyfriend, Clinton Bolton.

Dominique had been working on private boats for many years. At twenty-eight, she could navigate as well as prepare and present a banquet for twenty. She had the skills and determination to more than qualify her as a navigator or mechanic as well. We had cruised many offshore miles together, and she was aboard when I brought *Bagan* from California through the Panama Canal and up to Rhode Island. She was more than qualified to do The Passage and I was more than anxious to have her help the effort. During that trip from California to Rhode Island, Clinton joined us in the Bahamas and helped bring *Bagan* the final leg up the East Coast to my home port of Newport.

During that trip, I got to know Clinton, learn about his impressive boating history, and observe how he and Dominique worked together on a boat. By the time we reached Newport, I knew that this was a team I needed to ensure successful transit through The Passage. Clinton would run the boat side of the project, Dominique the domestic.

When we returned in the summer of 2007, I was using *Bagan* as a floating production facility and research center for an underwater archeological group I had been working with for the past three-plus years. At the time, the Rhode Island Marine Archeological Project (RIMAP) was conducting underwater research trying to find and identify various ships that had been sunk in and around Newport during the American Revolution. Despite a rigorous schedule of diving and filming underwater, the Northwest Passage project was ever present in my mind.

In my off hours, I tried to find further funding and support. Securing the needed extra funding was a problem, and getting the word out into the media was an uphill battle. But the enthusiasm from those around me for the six-month Northwest Passage trip was encouraging.

One night in September 2007, I had dinner with Dominique and Clinton and presented the idea of the trip to them, asking them to join the project and help get *Bagan* and her potential crew prepared for the trip of a lifetime.

I was met with neutral stares from both of them, not quite registering what I was presenting. Dominique actually laughed, thinking it was a joke. I had to stress to both of them several times that I was serious, that I truly felt that with both of their wonderful offshore experiences and work ethics,

Dominique and Clinton were the only two people who could help me pull this off.

At this point, I took my first of many gambles. With only a handshake on the funding from Nordhavn, I offered them full-time positions, starting a year later in the summer of 2008, proposing to pay them weekly for their work aboard *Bagan* to upgrade and prep her for the trip. Once we left the docks of Newport and started to head to The Passage, I'd pay them their full salary in advance.

I couldn't afford to lose them while waiting for Nordhavn's promised money, so I started to dig into my own cash. I had recently sold a house in California and was now attacking the profit I made from that sale. Clinton and Dominique picked up on my excitement and eagerly signed on. The two of them, who were perhaps some of the very best in their fields, agreed to greatly reduced salaries.

Not finding a yard in Newport that was willing to help us by cutting us a break on winter storage, Dominique and Clinton took *Bagan* to Stamford, Connecticut, where the boat would be stored indoors and worked on during the winter of 2008–09.

That fall, Dominique and Clinton began their work by tearing down all the ship's systems and assessing them on a basic "Excellent Condition/Replace Condition" basis; if they were even slightly suspect, we'd replace them. Working off the premise that we would truly be on our own up there, hundreds if not thousands of miles from help, we started to buy backup parts for all the systems: impellers, water pumps, fuel pumps, wing-engine and generator, diesel injectors, belts, alternators, filters, hydraulic hoses, pressure valves, domestic water pumps, bilge pumps, holding tank pumps, emergency underwater epoxy to patch a hole if the ice should breech the fiberglass hull, and even a spare 500-pound propeller.

I hooked up Dominique with Dr. Phil Wagner and between them they assembled a ship's medical kit. From Phil, Dominique learned everything from setting a broken arm to inserting and hanging an IV drip. During that winter, Dominique and Clinton found a cheap sublet in Connecticut, which I rented for them to save them the two-hour commute from Rhode Island.

Despite their efforts at economizing, I was slowly beginning to leak growing amounts of cash—personal cash.

I also knew that I would need someone to help with the filming. I wanted to bring back rarely seen underwater footage, so I needed to find a diver willing to give me a very large chunk of time, perhaps without pay, who understood freezing water temperatures and its special equipment needs, and who would be able to live in a small, contained area for vast amounts of time with no real break.

Greg DeAscentis fit all three requirements. I'd first met Greg many years earlier when I'd started diving with RIMAP. He was a no-nonsense diver with great concern for history and the environment. Greg holds a college degree in anthropology and both he and his wife, Laura, are wonderful photographers. During those years, Greg ran the small dive boat that RIMAP used to dive on the Revolutionary War era wrecks. From his boat-handling to his diving skills to his skill with a wrench, Greg was exactly what I needed.

Within days I'd presented my plan to him. After giving it a few seconds' thought he wholeheartedly agreed to join.

To help round out the crew, I knew that for at least a leg or two of the trip I wanted my twenty-two-year-old son Sefton aboard. Sefton and I had done a fair amount of boating together and I'd watched him grow from a young guy learning the ropes to a young man who needed few instructions when it came to the everyday running of the boat. He wasn't quite a pro in the field yet but he had unwavering enthusiasm and an ability to grasp new ideas quickly. Aside from simply wanting to share this upcoming experience with him, I could truly use his help. He agreed to come.

What was slowly brewing beneath the surface was the fact that in 1992, when Sefton was five and his half-sister Dominique eleven, I went through a bad divorce. At the time we were all living in Los Angeles and I was working as an actor. Sadly, the pressures of the entertainment industry as well as a basic mismatch in personalities between my wife and me brought on the divorce. For the past fifteen years, we'd never spent much time together as a family. After the divorce, they moved back to Michigan where my ex-wife's family was, and then eventually to Colorado.

At the time of the divorce, I was strongly urged by my attorney to seek sole custody of Sefton. Knowing that this would rip the family apart, I fired my attorney and sought joint custody, my ex-wife being the custodial parent. I remained in Los Angeles, eventually moving back to Rhode Island.

I'd been with Sefton many times and in all the years he had lived happily with Dominique, his half-brother Chauncey, and his mom, but all three kids and I were rarely together. Despite the best intentions and efforts of all, this was simply a very sad fact of life and we did our best to adjust. As a parent, I'll go to my grave hoping I did the best but feeling it was never quite enough.

Signing up Dominique and Sefton for such a trip was a step in the right direction, yet it wasn't as easy with my thirty-one-year-old stepson Chauncey. The family divorce couldn't help but cause great pain and disillusionment. It took many years of hard work and painful communication between Dominique and me to come to terms, for her to express her pain, and for me to explain the thinking process behind the split.

For reasons that I can only guess, Chauncey never took up the invitation to try to work through it, and it caused great pain for both of us. I don't think we actually had a real conversation or any form of communication after the divorce. The oldest of his siblings, Chauncey struck out early to find his way in the world. I had always hoped that despite the distance, the original thread of love was there and that there would indeed be a time when we could all be together.

In early September 2008, Dan, Jim from Nordhavn, and I flew to Canada and joined an icebreaker in Cambridge Bay, a small Inuit town in the heart of The Passage. Cambridge Bay is well above the Arctic Circle and 1,500 miles south of the North Pole. With a population of approximately 1,400, it is the largest town in The Passage. It's a maintenance base for the area's line of DEW (Distant Early Warning) stations that remain in place since the heated tensions of the Cold War.

Cambridge Bay also hosts a group of working geologists, as well as the starting point for the 385-foot ship, *Akademik Ioff*, now a passenger-carrying ship that at one point was part of Russia's Cold War fleet. *Akademik Ioff* would be home for two weeks of Arctic exploring, a tenth of the time I was planning aboard *Bagan*, following approximately the same route (not counting the 3,000 miles it'd take to get to The Passage and, once through, the 3,000 miles it'd take to get to Seattle).

The days quickly rolled by as Dan, Jim, and I experienced the frigid waters of The Passage. Perhaps twice a day we'd join other passengers in twenty-foot inflatable boats and explore the vast and barren lands around us.

All the while I was shooting video to get generic footage to show potential sponsors what I was hoping to do. Each night we'd gather at the dinner table and discuss what we'd need to do in the next nine months as well as how much money it would take and when the money would be needed.

The main purpose of our trip on *Akademik Ioff* was to find out the physical feasibility of our intended joint expedition and to see what the ice conditions were like. For me, I hoped to gain a good visual sense of what I'd be trying to capture on film. Within the first few days, I knew I would bring back never-before-seen footage from The Passage. From Dan and Jim's perspective, they grew confident that a Nordhavn boat could take on The Passage and survive. Each morning, the crew of *Akademik Ioff* provided the ship's passengers with its own newspaper, giving the latest headlines. Each morning, the three of us would sit and discuss the sorry case of the world in general and feel all the more secure that our intended trip through the Northwest Passage was about as timely as we could hope for.

On September 15, 2008, with a growing sense of accomplishment and anticipation, I sat down for breakfast and opened the ship's daily newspaper. I stared in abject and total disbelief at the latest headlines noting that Lehman Brothers was crashing, about to be financially erased from the face of the earth, and that the collateral damage was going to be unprecedented.

The collateral damage reached the Far North. As the days continued to roll by, Jim no longer wanted to discuss the trip. In fact, Jim no longer ate with Dan and me. When the three of us actually were together, the talk was of anything but their $300,000 commitment to the trip and perhaps building a forty-foot boat so they could join in the adventure. By the time the trip aboard *Akademik Ioff* had ended, there was no $300,000 commitment. I saw it coming a mile away.

Dan Streech was the type of man who, when he told me of the offer's withdrawal, he did it with tears in his eyes. I was completely in Dan's corner. I couldn't in good conscience ask for such a large amount of money while he was looking at having to lay off longtime trusted employees, people he truly loved.

But as much as I appreciated Dan's position and honesty, I was devastated. Actually, more than devastated. I was completely and decisively screwed.

CHAPTER 2

THREE STEPS FORWARD, TWO STEPS SIDEWAYS

By the end of 2008, I was already into the trip for about $100,000 out of my own pocket and was still anxiously awaiting the first check from Nordhavn—which would never be coming. I had hired screenwriter Marc Rosenberg, director Adam Weismann, and part-time cinematographer Ulli Bonnekamp, who would be aboard to film the second and most beautiful leg, Halifax to Greenland.

Added to my daily to-do/wish list were fervent hopes and prayers that something, anything would come up. As the economy continued to collapse, the bills kept coming: gear for the boat, gear for the crew, flights into and out of various ports, food, charts and unexpected problems with the boat's hidden "soft" systems, such as water pressure pumps, the heating system, or a garbage disposal. Lugging around full garbage bags in a polar bear-infested land was not an option.

The expedition's website soaked up money like a proverbial sponge. If the trip were to stand a chance—any chance—I needed to get the word out, but to whom?

The fact that Nordhavn had to pull funding showed that the idea of making cold calls, approaching companies where I had no connection for support, was a non-starter. Not only were calls not returned, they simply weren't accepted.

I was starting to hemorrhage money. I'd already given the writer and cinematographer advances. If I backed down now or tried to skip corners with either of these two, I'd run the very real risk of having a less-than-perfect project to deliver. I had also advanced money to Dominique and Clinton.

As we plummeted into the dead of winter in 2009, I had crossed the $200,000 line. My spending was only starting. I did have one ace up my sleeve that truly made the difference between the trip coming to fruition or not.

What was once a very healthy savings account was now looking more like a young child's passbook account. And it was going fast. It was at this time I also needed to tend to a few nagging health issues.

Enter "The Toe From Hell."

Two years before, when Dominique and I had brought *Bagan* around from California, I was delayed in La Paz, Mexico, for emergency arthroscopic knee surgery. An MRI showed that over the years, I had torn about 90 percent of the meniscus in one knee and that about 20 percent of the damaged tissue was now floating around freely under my kneecap. It also showed that my "good" knee had suffered about 80 percent damage. The accident that led to the surgery happened while I was filming hammerhead sharks, perhaps one of ocean's shyest creatures. Forty miles off La Paz, in 200 feet of water, there is a sea mount known as El Baho that hosts a community of up to twenty of these amazing sharks. At the end of the day during one of these filming trips, I was climbing back aboard the dive boat with underwater camera gear in hand when my right knee simply exploded. It felt as though a nest of maniacal hornets had been let loose just under my kneecap, jamming my leg in the extended position.

After several months of rehab we left La Paz aboard *Bagan* on April 1, 2007 and started our way down to the Panama Canal. In Costa Rica, I had to make a leap from *Bagan* to the dock. Trying to protect my still-healing knee, I landed awkwardly on the wrong foot, breaking my little toe. Normally this would not be a big deal, but in this case, over the months, it turned into one.

The toe healed, but the accident left a tiny but bothersome bone chip in the joint. It was intermittently painful, more annoying than anything, but it eventually wore me down. I figured that if I was going to be in the Arctic for months, everything in my body had better be in as good a working order as all the boat's systems. I decided to have the bone chip removed and, in early 2009, I had surgery in New York.

While the good doctor and I were gauzed up and sterilized, I couldn't help but notice the layers of dust on his air conditioner. Things weren't as sanitary as one would hope for, but he was the doctor and I was simply the paying patient.

Two weeks later, I went back to him with pain and swelling and a dark purple toe. "It's supposed to look like that," he said.

I quickly made an appointment with Dr. Marty O'Malley at New York's Hospital for Special Surgery. He assured me it was indeed not supposed to look like that, ordered an MRI, and immediately found a bone infection. Within days, I was under the knife at HSS, a second operation on this tiny and seemingly useless digit. Two weeks later the pain started again. Despite the amount of painkillers I slammed back, it always felt as though the surgeon's knife was still tearing up my toe. Dr. O'Malley ordered another MRI and there, again, was yet another bone infection. A week later, I went under the knife again. Dr. O'Malley did what he could, drilled out the bone, removed the infection, sewed me up, and once more sent me on my way. Within three weeks, the toe exploded again into a burning, purple lump. Marty is one of the very best doctors I've ever had. He's fun, charismatic, concerned, and no bullshit. When I went back to him for the third time, he simply looked at it and said, "I've done all I can do. We need to go to the next level." It was then that I was sent to an Infectious Disease specialist who, after looking at the history of this Toe From Hell, ordered me on an IV antibiotic drip for six weeks, a portable IV drip that I was to self-administer twice a day for an hour at a time.

By then it was mid-April, and we were within two months of departure for our 8,500-mile odyssey. Between the disappearing funds and Hell Toe, things were not looking good at all.

The antibiotics were leaving me beaten up and constantly feeling sea-sick. Clinton at one point asked Dominique, "He looks like shit. Is he going to be able to do this trip?" Most days I needed at least two naps and by evening I was unable to do anything but attach my drip and fall asleep. Despite all the antibiotics pumped into me, my pain increased, making it hard even to sleep, and I felt as though I was undergoing the toe surgery with no anesthesia—brutal, searing, hot pain. There was no way I was going to be able to lug cameras around the Canadian Arctic or dive under the ice to get footage with this damn infected toe. I tried to keep this new development to myself as much as I could.

The planned departure date, June 14, 2009, continued to rush towards us, the bills still pouring in, the economy continuing its free fall, and the project's financial drain and unexpected problems ceaselessly mounting. I'd come to the conclusion that no company in its right fiscal mind was going to help with the funding. There was little let up. Daily, Dominique was buying and stocking *Bagan* with almost two tons of food; vacuum sealed and frozen packages of stew meats, hundreds of cans of tuna, chicken, ham, turkey, boxes of rice, cereal, coffee, tea, UHT milk (milk in a box, like Parmalat), cans of juice, canned vegetables, bags of potatoes, bread, and pounds of cheese.

Knowing that we would face days, if not weeks and perhaps months, of conditions so bad that frying an egg would be extremely challenging, Dominique cooked dozens of hearty meals ahead of time and froze them. She did an amazing job, but food was costing thousands of dollars. My credit cards were getting friction burns.

We still had to buy our protection for the Arctic—the guns and ammunition would cost us $3,000. I finally faced the reality and started selling old production equipment so I could buy new audio equipment, tape stock, backup hard drives, a microphone, and cables.

By now *Bagan* was brought up from Stamford to Newport and was at the docks of The Goat Island Marina, one of the few entities that saw our plight and gave us a break in dock price. Goat Island was perfect, offering parking and storage for our gear. The marina boasts a very long and proud maritime history, with many of the transatlantic races ending there. Several around-the-world races sailed out of Goat Island at one point.

Six weeks prior to departure, I was notified that due to an ex-account-ant's mistake, I lost an IRS audit for $12,000. Then the medical bills started coming in. The project was morphing from a hoped-for documentary into a nightmarish Fellini film.

It was during this time that an expected but nonetheless very emotional event momentarily stopped me cold. Two years earlier, I had separated from my second wife, Kim, whom I'd married in 1998. Since this was a trip that could very possibly have a deadly outcome, I had urged Kim to file for legal separation. The papers were due to arrive a few weeks before we were to leave. While in the back of my mind I knew it was coming, the reality of a once-happy marriage ending was a powerfully sad realization. I really did not want this in the forefront of my consciousness while working my way through the ice-bound Arctic. The failing of the marriage was something I knew I had to look at and come to painful terms with in the months to come. What made it even worse was the fact that this was going to be my second divorce.

By this time, spring was making itself known in the usual Newport fash-ion and as *Bagan* became heavier and heavier with gear and sat lower on her lines, the May winds howled around her at the dock, offering a suggestion of things to come.

Around the same time I received the legal papers from Kim, I received a short text from Clinton, "Hope yr sitting dwn." *Bagan's* all-important water-maker system hadn't survived the winter despite the very expensive indoor storage at the yard.

The damage occurred on one of those brutally cold winter weekends, a weekend that, unbeknownst to me, Clinton was in Florida, racing. Clinton was able to work a local company down to $14,000 to replace the system.

Prior to departure, Sandy Davies, a marine electronics genius from Connecticut, reported that *Bagan* would need a whole new computer and satellite system. Two weeks before departure, Sandy's guys as well as other vendors were aboard *Bagan* installing new electronic components and satellite domes. It was paramount that I would be able to upload blogs, articles, and pictures during the trip. I'd been contracted by Peter Janssen of *Motor-Boating* magazine for a series of articles that I was to write and upload as the trip progressed. I was also hoping to update the website on a somewhat regular basis, tasks that worked well at the docks of Newport but could become difficult above the Arctic Circle. Then there were the potential sponsors. After we'd sent out our brutally expensive PR and media kits, they wouldn't even accept our calls. As the cliché goes, in for a penny, in for a pound. But I wasn't going to go down without a fight. To meet the financial tsunami, I began selling, at a tremendous loss, some of my long-held stocks, worrying about capital losses later.

In order to raise cash to meet the needs of the latest round of bills, I bid on some infomercial-type jobs. I tried to form a non-profit to attract potential donors but was, at the eleventh hour, denied by the IRS. It was financial death by a thousand cuts.

My resolve was starting to weaken. If I called off the trip now I'd lose less than if I completely ran out of money weeks prior to our scheduled June departure.

Dominique and Clinton dropped by my apartment for our weekly pizza meeting. We pored over lists, they handed over receipts, and we discussed where we were. I was now thinking about bailing out and cutting my losses, but this was as harrowing and gut-wrenching as thinking about staying the course. Sleep had been impossible for months. My health (mental as well as physical) was borderline. I had a crew looking to me with great excitement and hope to take them north while I watched the world's economy going south.

I finally came to the conclusion that the trip was wrong. I was headed for financial ruin. If I was to have anything in the way of a stable future, I should take the loss and move on.

And then, inspiration struck.

Several bank stocks that I'd seen plummet started to show something vaguely resembling heartbeats. Bank of America, in particular, was fluttering. I didn't know the first thing about day trading but I had a rough idea about how it worked. I dabbled at first. I bought small amounts of these bank stocks and sold them days later after they rose a point or two. I'd watch them fall back down again and would roll my profits into them, grabbing anywhere from half a point to two points. I got braver and braver, more emboldened and blind to the downside.

Out of sheer desperation, I started to buy large amounts with what money I had left in the budget. One day I secured enough profit to buy us diesel from Newport to Halifax; another day I gained a small profit that could help acquire the necessary charts, and on and on until I finally lost my nerve. It wasn't pretty, but thanks to the world's very respected, revered, and legalized form of gambling, I was able to repair some of the project's fiscal damage to the tune of about $15,000 in quick profits.

Yet it wasn't all doom and gloom for the future of the trip. About a month before our projected departure date of June 14, 2009, I received an unexpected email from my stepson, Chauncey.

Through Dominique and Sefton, Chauncey had learned about the project and became intrigued. He has always been a man of the outdoors. He spent many years competing on the professional snowboarding circuit and with the help of several sponsors such as Helly Hansen, Burton, and Oakley, was able to eke out a living and win several championships.

Whether it was half-pipe or downhill, there wasn't much that Chauncey wouldn't tackle, a bold attitude that eventually resulted in his breaking several bones as well as his jaw. In his spare time, he was an avid hiker of the backcountry of Colorado. He and Sefton both held passion for the outdoors and, given the chance, wouldn't miss the opportunity to try to stretch their horizons. Chauncey had been saddled in the real world for the past few years and had put his business degree from the University of Colorado to use working for UBS in Denver.

He'd emailed me with the news that UBS was going through a shakeup and a good deal of their employees were being offered incentives to leave, perhaps a nice way of saying that a mass firing was in the air. Chauncey said he was thinking of taking advantage of their offer and that, if needed, he was available to help prep the boat for the trip, gratis. His offer was one of the very few that came without any strings or hidden agendas attached and it didn't require a lot of thought to take him up on it. I told him I'd love to have him come.

It also presented a wonderful opportunity for us to spend some time together for a few weeks and perhaps take a look at a few fences in need of mending. Chauncey and Dominique's father, Yves Marie Tanton, lives in Newport and over the years, their visits to him had been catalysts for our getting together, something that Dominique and I were able to take advantage of, but for reasons unknown, Chauncey and I never were.

I've always regarded Dominique and Chauncey as far more than step-children and knew that a part of me could never rest until we were all back on the same page.

So much was our love for each other that when Dominique was eight years old, she was heard to mumble to herself, "Sprague married Mom so that I could be his stepdaughter," which was very close to the truth. I fervently wished that Chauncey's offer to help was going to be a first step in bringing me, Chauncey, Dominique, and Sefton together, and it lifted my beaten spirits to no end.

When Chauncey arrived, he dove into the work. With Sefton's arrival a week later, *Bagan* became an object of very determined family attention.

Everyone worked twelve- to fifteen-hour days, freeing me up to tend to my job—check-writer. Find money and spend it before the next four bills arrived. It was said that Amundsen left Norway waving goodbye to a dock full of creditors, a scenario I was trying desperately to avoid but was moving closer and closer to every day.

As we approached June 14, it was becoming apparent that we wouldn't be ready. Tensions were rapidly mounting. If experience has taught me anything, it is to avoid a hasty departure and honor the old but powerful sailor's superstition, never leave on a Friday.

Part of the original goal I'd presented to Clinton was that I wanted the boat ready two weeks prior to departure so that we wouldn't leave with an energy or sleep deficit. But now we were facing the very thing I wanted to avoid. As much as I hated to do it, I postponed the departure from Newport for a day. And then for another day. I realized that as long as we stayed tied to the docks of Goat Island, our to-do lists would continue to grow and problems continue to pop up. With little fanfare, I announced that, ready or not, we were leaving June 16, period.

The three-day leg to Halifax would act as our shakedown cruise. As we prepared to leave, Chauncey and Sefton had to let go of the project and fly back to Denver. Their help in the past few weeks had been immeasurable and their spirits motivating. Sadly, I said good-bye to both, but at least I knew that I'd be seeing Sefton since he was still aiming to do the Greenland-to-Barrow, Alaska, leg.

Sefton's studies at the University of Colorado, Denver didn't allow for him to do much more than that but he was going to be along for the actual Passage itself. Chauncey, on the other hand, had helped us as much as he could.

On June 15, miracles started to occur. Whether it be God, Yahweh, Allah, or some other deity of your choice, his or her work is always at hand. For me at least, it sometimes takes a powerful shaking for the higher power to get my attention. I'd been focusing on the actual and successful transiting of the Northwest Passage for so long that I didn't see what had been in front of me for the past month. I'd been fretting and worrying about the finances so much that I was the last to see what had started to develop. Just prior to his

departure, Sefton decided that he would delay the first semester of his soph-
omore year at U of C. If there was room and if I wanted him along, he'd do
the entire trip—all the way to Seattle.

Shortly before his departure back to Colorado, Chauncey took me
aside and said that the past two weeks had been second to none and that
with all his heart he wished he could do some of the trip.

He offered nothing more than a great work ethic and wonderful sense
of humor, my two main requirements out of life. Later that night, I presented his joining us to Dominique. Never mind whether or not we could
afford it, but did we have the capacity to carry the extra food needed? To the
rest of the crew I asked if they could handle an extra person for the 8,500
miles. To a person they said yes. It was my very happy job to let Chauncey
know that if he could manage it, we'd love him to come along for the en-
tirety of the expedition.

Very suddenly, the scope and nature of the trip changed radically for
me. While we were still planning on doing what only a handful of boats had
managed to do since 1906, we were now a family that, for the first time in
almost fifteen years, was going to be back together, at least for the duration
of the trip. Dominique would make the entire trip; Sefton would come
aboard in Halifax and remain until the end; and Chauncey would join us in
Sisimiut, Greenland, and he, too, would stay until the very end.

Four people who were separated more than a decade and a half ago were
now being given the rare opportunity to reconnect and perhaps start anew.
June 16, 2009, dawned with a deep blue New England sky. A fresh, morning
breeze out of the northwest played about *Bagan* and gently bumped her up
against what might be one of her last secure resting places for the next five
months. Her tired crew quietly stowed last-minute items and double-
checked deck lashings and safety devices for events and places no one could
predict or, as of yet, imagine. As the small crew scurried about silently, an
invisible transition was occurring. After waiting for two years, *Bagan* was
now ready to lead the way into a vast and deadly unknown.

The docks at Goat Island were virtually empty. Those few who did saunter by took little notice of *Bagan* or her crew. At 11:00 a.m., 103 years to the day after Amundsen's ship *Gjoa* left Oslo, *Bagan's* 325-horsepower Lugger diesel engine was fired up in earnest and, with little fanfare, she slipped her lines.

As we slowly powered through Newport's inner harbor, I picked up my cell phone and called Pierre Irving, a very dear sailing friend in Newport. Pierre and I had shared many hard-fought miles together, The Two Man Transatlantic Race in particular being some of our toughest. I wanted to call and simply say good-bye to him and his wife, Kathy.

Bagan made her way out of the harbor entrance, past Ft. Adams and Goat Island landmarks that I'd known and honored for years, landmarks that I was starting to realize I may never see again.

Not near his phone, Pierre's outgoing voicemail message played. As it did, the enormity of what lay ahead of us hit me—8,500 miles through some of the world's harshest maritime environment. The concept of navigating uncharted waters and as yet unknown perils to cross from the Atlantic to the Pacific swept over me and I couldn't speak.

As Pierre's voicemail beeped, my tears kept me from leaving the simplest of messages. I merely wanted to say that I'd see them in five months and wanted to wish them a wonderful summer.

I couldn't.

The overwhelming thought of what my summer and fall held choked off any words. I wasn't ready for it but unintentionally I'd severed the last connection to home and could only pray that we were ready for what lay ahead.

CHAPTER 3

HALIFAX SHAKEDOWN

"Farewell to the lovely girls of Newport."

These were among the first words in Captain John Boit's ship's log, the *Union,* of August 1794. At the tender age of nineteen, Boit was a full captain and was to become the first man to sail a crewed sloop around the world. Two years later, the sloop *Union* and crew arrived in Boston with crew and ship intact, unheard of in those days. Through the years, I'd always marveled at Boit's accomplishment. A distant relative, Boit's voyage held a grip on me.

Undeniably it was in my blood and there was never any doubt that I was always drawn to that which I couldn't see. I needed to know the whys and wherefores of what couldn't easily be explained. This basic curiosity manifested itself for me in boats and storm-tossed horizons. It clearly was a trait that drove me on these past few years with determination and focus.

But that very trait was slowly now beginning to show its dark side.

As we made our way down Narragansett Bay, I thought of the world Boit had left behind and what he was expecting, fearing, and hoping to encounter. I quickly found that all thoughts of romanticism, reflecting back on proud family moments or simply acknowledging the similarities in our adventures—faded quickly. What grabbed full control of my attention that bright and beautiful summer day was the nagging question that kept me up the better part of the past two nights:

"What in God's name was I doing?"

For the most part, the lists had been crossed off, food bought, *Bagan* prepped as well as she's ever been, charts purchased, research done—all with no expenses spared. Yet, for the past forty-eight hours, I was starting to question the very sanity of the trip: who was I to ask these collected crew members to put their lives on the line with a less-than-good chance that all would work out as I'd planned?

Up until this point, I'd tried my best to avoid detractors and negative thinking. I did whatever I could to find the positives and move ahead. It is a personal philosophy I've been trying to live by for the past thirty-one years and, to some degree, it has worked.

Standing atop *Bagan*'s flying bridge as she started her trip down through Narragansett Bay and up to the Cape Cod Canal, I found that morning that I simply couldn't feel the overriding optimism I was counting on to drive me for the next five months. The pressures to succeed on such an expedition are indescribable; their strength and persistence far greater than any one person can handle. This project had been underway for eighteen months and while I'd surrounded myself with the very best crew and ground support I could find, the pressures were absolutely inexorable.

Now the crew and their fate hung over me. We were heading offshore as prepared as we could possibly be and with the utmost latest in safety, training, and medical gear, but the feeling that I held four other lives in the palm of my hand was as unsettling as anything I've ever experienced. Just because I'm willing to undertake a project that holds a very strong element of the unthinkable, what gave me the right to take four others into the same scenario? I was tired and terrified that I'd lost the flame.

Sliding past Castle Hill light, one of the great landmarks of Newport, *Bagan* coursed her way northeast across Buzzard's Bay in a slight chop with fair winds from the southwest. We had perhaps one-foot seas on the beam, coming in from the south, and *Bagan* was taking this in a way I've never before felt. With more than two tons aboard, she sliced through the chop with power, strength, and grace. The engine was all but jogging, moving us along at a steady seven knots with little concern. Preliminary trips to the engine room showed that all the work and prep that we'd done down there was paying off: no leaks, no smells, and all temperatures in their expected zones.

As we headed northeast to the Canal, I watched as the region's classic sailboats worked their courses over Buzzard's Bay. I took great comfort in watching those beautiful wooden hulls being driven through the water by sails drawn and built decades before.

Later that cool summer evening, as we exited the Cape Cod Canal and entered the Gulf of Maine, Clinton and I were on watch in the pilothouse, and Dominique was aft in the galley, still stowing and arranging food and trying to crank out our first official dinner at sea.

Clinton and I were seated in the secure and sturdy helm seats, discussing the crossing of the gulf and planned arrival time at Halifax. What we suddenly saw before us was incomprehensible, if not gut-wrenching. Both of the ship's computer monitors showed the "blue screen of death" and went blank. We sat in stunned silence. The scramble of the last five days as well as the draining amount I had to pay to have the computer upgraded and properly programmed immediately seemed for naught. My mind raced ahead to nowhere. Grave concerns ricocheted around in my head like lightning strikes, my stomach immediately seized up into its now all-too-familiar ball of stress, a piece of cold granite.

My first comprehensible thought was, "How much will this cost and which credit card isn't maxed out?" We said nothing as Clinton dove under the console and tried to reboot the now dead computer tower. I just had to sit and watch and do my best not to register the almost debilitating concern that was coursing through my system.

To try and gain perspective, I walked outside onto the deck and tried to enjoy a beautiful summer sunset. I found I could take little solace in the beauty of the familiar shorelines and muted colors around me. I watched as the evening sun bathed the local folks on the banks fishing. It was a studied contrast. Here they were, seemingly without a care in the world, depending on the basics of rod and reel. And here we were on our way to great exploration through desolate areas of the Arctic, depending on modern technology and soulless electronics.

School was never easy for me. Add to the fact that in those days the school at which I spent second through ninth grade, The Potomac School in Virginia, was a strict place that had no tolerance for students with different learning styles. It was a place as close to a living hell as I can remember.

During those years, I was referred to as "dumb," "lazy," and/or "not motivated," and was singled out for "not trying." I was coarsely lectured, humiliated, and most damagingly shamed time and again before my peers. Potomac called me just about everything but what I was—dyslexic.

To this day, if the number "41" is put before me, more than half the time I'll see it as "14." You can tell me that the number is forty-one and after closer and more precise examination I'll see it as such. And because of the pressures of flipping numbers, I often hear the opposite of what's being said.

At age twelve, I had found alcohol and drugs. By the time I was fourteen, self-medication was a way of life for me and, once I started, I didn't have a straight day for the next dozen years. It was at age 27 that life turned for me; whether it was an act of God, Buddha, or some other higher power, something on the morning of July 3, 1978, had me reaching out to the phone (the only thing I had in my one-room apartment that wasn't broken, booze-stained or puke-stained) and calling AA.

That evening was my first AA meeting and, for the past thirty-three years, I have been free (I certainly won't say trouble-free) of a lifestyle and attitude that were quickly destroying me. I guess in one manner I should thank Potomac School for properly heading me out onto the path of self-destruction for it brought me to a life that I never in my wildest dreams thought I'd be living.

And therein was the ultimate problem with our current computer crash. I knew that, in theory, Clinton and/or I could manage plotting our way for the next five months using paper charts, but this was a task I didn't know if I was up for or not. I could do it and had done it successfully for years but the lack of confidence with numbers and my second-guessing provided great stress and effort, two things I'd been living with daily for the past two years.

Aboard for the leg to Halifax was Ted Croy. Apart from his many skills, Ted was also a computer maven. At age fifteen, he actually built his first home computing system. It didn't take long for Ted to come up with a possible diagnosis: the computer wasn't strong enough to handle the multiple programs demanding so much all at once. Knowing that I was about to take yet another in a growing list of massive financial hits, I asked Ted what he'd suggest. He put pencil to paper and a few minutes later told me we'd need a gaming computer and a powerful one at that.

It was turning into my personal mantra, or at least motto, for the trip but "in for a penny, in for a pound" was all I could think. A new computer wasn't going to be cheap. Add to that I was going to need Sandy in Connecticut to build it. Since he was the person who originally installed its programs, he knew best what we needed. Then there was going to be the shipping to Canada and Customs to deal with when we arrived.

Trying to put all worries aside and place my full trust in Clinton and Ted's advice, I rotated out of watch and headed for my cabin. I had the "master cabin," which offered a queen bunk and private head. Sefton and I were to share this cabin but until his arrival it was all mine and I planned on taking full advantage of the privacy and peace—the fact notwithstanding that the engine wasn't two feet away from me aft in the engine room.

With gentle rocking of the hull and the ever-present loud droning of the 325-horsepower engine, I was quickly lulled to sleep only to be awoken what seemed like minutes later for my watch. I was told all was well, weather was holding, and the computer seemed okay. After grabbing a quick mug of black tea, I took my place in the pilothouse, settled in, and very quickly heard the dreaded sound of the engine "spooling up" (running quickly) and then dying. My immediate fear was that we'd picked up something in the prop and, with fifty-eight-degree water, going over the side wasn't something

I was looking forward to doing. Within seconds, Clinton was up from his cabin and without saying a word we both immediately headed down to the engine room. We hemmed and hawed, poked and prodded, and very quickly came up with the conclusion that we'd sucked a tank dry.

Bagan holds 2,000 gallons of diesel and carries it in four tanks, two forward and two aft. We'd been running off one of the forward tanks ever since the boat left Connecticut months back and, in a nutshell, that tank was now dry. I'm not sure why the tank wasn't topped off before we left Newport but I imagine it was due to hoped-for-better fuel costs in Canada. The tank level was something I thought Clinton was on top of and I guess he felt that it was something I was monitoring. Regardless where the oversight lay, we quickly bled the engine of air, switched tanks, and in a matter of moments were underway again. Oddly, I came away from this experience with the slight feeling that the responsibility for this mini-mess was mine.

Holding the good weather and nursing the ship's computer system, two days later we arrived in Halifax and tied up to the docks of The Royal Nova Scotia Yacht Squadron. Tucked back in the still, cold Canadian waters and surrounded by a forest of tall, lush evergreens, we settled *Bagan* onto the floating wooden docks and immediately set about contacting Sandy, explaining to him what had happened with the computer, and letting him know what we were thinking. He quickly set to building the required system but not before I sent a check for $5,000. Sandy is one of the best at what he does and I trusted him implicitly, a trust which stood me well through the next five months. While the cost was heartbreaking, I knew that Sandy was doing his best.

Clinton called Customs and there we sat waiting for them to come down to the boat, check passports, and clear us into Canada, something that, being a child of the '60s, always has me a bit on edge and concerned. One of the many luxuries of hiring Clinton for the trip was that as the official captain, the clearing into and out of countries was his responsibility and all I had to do was sit back and not look defensive—or guilty, neither of which I had cause to be. When pressed with "officialdom," I always try to present a large smile couched in as much cooperation as possible. After the usual paperwork and questions, the Customs officers politely and efficiently cleared us into Canada and headed off up the bare wooden docks with our paperwork—and guns. Realizing the potential of what we might be facing once we were up in the Arctic, we'd made sure to have the necessary guns and ammunition for protection. Polar bears were our main concern. I knew that if it ever came down to it, having to shoot a charging polar bear would be an act of very low returns. I'm not a big fan of hunting, and while I appreciate the sport and effort behind it, it has never been an appealing choice for me. I can, however, say that, unlike the feelings of a few onboard, it would not be an easy or straightforward choice to simply "drop him in his tracks."

What I learned from my time on the Russian icebreaker ten months earlier was that the best defense was to shoot several concussion rounds at a bear's feet and hope to drive him off with a good scare. In Halifax, we were warned in no-uncertain terms by a man who had spent many days in Canada's Arctic that, "If you see a polar bear, you'd best understand that he's been hunting you for half an hour. You don't just casually 'bump into' one of these killers."

This was moot since what we would hope to use in self-defense was now being carried up the docks by Canada's finest. We were assured of their return when we left Canada, all except the two .357 Magnum Desert Eagle semi-automatic handguns. Somewhere during preparations leading up to our departure, it was suggested to Clinton by one of the crew members, Greg, that we should have two handguns as well as the rifles and he knew where we could borrow them for the trip. Whether this concern and plan was ever passed along to me I can't remember. But I did know that by that point I had total trust in Clinton as our captain and if he felt the trip needed something, I agreed wholeheartedly.

It was also here in Halifax that we were to pick up our cinematographer, Ulli Bonnekamp, and Sefton. Here, too, in Halifax, we had to send Ted back to Rhode Island.

The arrival of my son, Sefton, was the beginning of what I hoped would be an overdue realization and admittance of past hurts, something which could lead to a wonderful road of healing for the both of us. My own father disappeared from my sister's life and mine when I was five. Our single-parent home was one fueled by excess drinking, with the sad specter of abuse always looming. The fact that Sefton and his siblings didn't have to face the uneasy feeling of never quite knowing what to expect from an alcohol-fueled crossing of personal boundaries went a long way to help make the painful aspect of divorce somewhat manageable, at least in my mind, when his mom and I split.

To this day, I'm not comfortable around those who drink excessively due to dealing with my own personal abuse of alcohol. (This distrust of drinkers would soon come to the fore and severely impact the trip.)

Sefton and I now faced four and a half uninterrupted months of a closeness very few fathers and sons would have the gift of sharing. We were coming into this with eyes wide open but, knowing that *Bagan* was going to be traveling the next 8,000 miles with Sefton, Dominique, Chauncey, and myself under the same roof, was far more exciting, intense, and challenging than the area we were hoping to transit. Through unpredictable and equally unbelievable means, now Sefton and Chauncey were going to be aboard (when Chauncey joined us in Greenland) and the family that had sadly dissolved not fifteen years earlier was going to be together for the first time.

The travel gods were all in sync because Ulli and Sefton arrived on the same night at Halifax's Stanfield International Airport. Unfortunately, the travel gods weren't entirely in sync as both airlines managed to lose both of their sets of luggage, which included the audio and camera gear Ulli needed for his three weeks aboard. I'd hired Ulli through a mutual friend in Los Angeles and while Ulli and I had never actually met face to face, we did have the chance to talk several times over the phone. The first time we talked I knew I liked him; he seemed gentle and affable. In our conversations, I was clear about what he could expect in regards to cramped, cold and stuffy shipboard life. He was equally clear about what gear he'd need and what salary he required.

We came to terms on it all. Ulli's work was superb; he'd won an Emmy, as had I. From what I could gather, he was very down to earth. He understood the pressures that we'd all be experiencing in a small boat and was game to start shooting (film, that is).

During our stay in Halifax, the special Arctic diving gear Greg had ordered was hung up by a bureaucratic snag. Despite numerous phone calls, the equipment was stalled at the border, then sent back to the States, a three-day process. During the same time, the new computer was likewise stalled.

On June 20, with textbook timing, the offshore winds started to swing out of the north, which would help to flatten the seas and allow us to start thinking about our next leg up Isle de la Madeleine to the Gulf of St. Lawrence. Also with perfect timing, Customs notified us that it would release the computer.

On the afternoon of June 25, in a developing fog and sloppy seas, we finally dropped our lines from the docks at Halifax and started out onto the next leg of what I hoped would continue to be a safe trip.

CHAPTER 4

ICEBERG BOUND

I raced formula cars for eight years—a dream at best, an expensive distraction at most. During that time, I bought more car parts than received trophies. While always looking to gain that extra tenth of a second, I learned many life lessons.

One was that rain was always the Great Equalizer. It didn't matter the horsepower or torque, racing in the rain gave everybody the same heavy disadvantage and the playing field was leveled.

In its own way, heavy thick and seemingly impenetrable offshore fog is the nautical equivalent of racing's Great Equalizer. Advanced electronics aren't 100 percent foolproof, and might make you see things that aren't there. Second-guessing your navigation is exhausting. We had been surrounded by deep fog for more than twenty-four hours. Dark shapes that wouldn't show up on radar seemed to appear, then disappear. Phantom sounds would taunt you.

I'm sure I once heard a dog bark mid-Atlantic.

We had been watching this fog from the safety of the docks at Halifax for several days. With time growing short, we felt that if we could loop far enough out into the Atlantic as we made our way northeast to the Canso Causeway, we could avoid most of the fog and stress. That wasn't to be, and we never truly shook it until we locked through the Causeway that separates cold, wet Atlantic from the sunny Gulf of St. Lawrence.

This leg had us all a bit off our game, still getting our sea legs. To make up for some of the time lost in Halifax, we powered through the night and dropped the hook the next morning at five, still in the fog, off the beach of Harve-Aubert, a small thriving island community in the southwest corner of The Gulf.

We all needed to stretch our legs, enjoy what the island had to offer, and work off stress from the fog. The time ashore would give Ulli a chance to work with the cameras, Clinton time to look at weather for the next leg to St. Anthony's, and the rest of us an opportunity to explore. I also needed to make calls and send emails to get a pulse back into the funding efforts. It was also a very good chance for all of us to build up some more energy reserves after the frenetic pace of the last week in Halifax.

The beauty of the multi-colored homes, small shops, and rolling green hills offered just the balm for us, and by day's end, we were once more back aboard *Bagan* and getting squared away for the crossing of Cabot Straights, then up the west side of Newfoundland. It was here that we would potentially start to encounter ice, a navigational impediment that we'd be dealing with for the unforeseeable future. The latest weather charts that we downloaded into the ship's computer showed a weakening high-pressure system that would provide us with ten to twelve knots of breeze with a slight chop. Dropping our lines at 10 a.m., we headed out and by 2 p.m., with steady tides pouring out of the Gulf of St. Lawrence, and a counter breeze from the south blowing against them, a sloppy combination of seas had developed. Our forecasted chop had 30-knot southerlies violently pushing against the tide creating between six- and ten-foot running seas.

It was at 3:05 p.m. that *Bagan* was put to her first test. We were all gathered in the pilothouse, which always provides comfort in bad weather. You can see how the boat handles the conditions.

And, of course, misery loves company.

In a set of three large waves, *Bagan* performed flawlessly, and a more-confident crew headed back to their stations. Clinton retook his helm seat and said to one and all, "We could have rolled back there, could have sunk." And there it sat. No one responded before he muttered, "I'd never seen so many white caps." In the last year, I'd had some terribly low moments during this project, yet I'd always pulled myself out, knowing that *Bagan* was eminently capable and my handpicked crew's experience and sense of hope and adventure was second to none. Yet in the flash of two relatively innocuous statements from our captain, my confidence in not only him but also the future of the trip could not have taken more of a hit. My mind raced quickly and tried to digest what Clinton had said. I went through any number of variables, but the one that pressed most heavily was, "Clinton isn't who he said he was."

Clinton had far more offshore miles than I did at that point, or so I was led to believe. I had about 40,000 miles under my belt and he easily had more. He had been a professional captain, successfully ran many boats, and had earned the respect of hundreds of crew and owners. Yet now in front of me was someone registering such alarm about an incident that didn't rate any higher on the "danger scale" than say a 5 out of 10. If those were his personal feelings, I had no real problem with it, except that what we may be facing in the months to come would potentially be out of Clinton's realm of experience. But the fact that he loudly announced to a very concerned crew that we "could have rolled" was unthinkable. Clinton had shown fear, and I was concerned.

In the coming 8,000 miles, we would face situations and challenges we couldn't have possibly conceived, forces of nature that in one instance snuffed out the lives of 126 sailors and two ships more than 100 feet long. I now had grave doubts about his leadership.

Shortly after leaving Newport, our twenty-foot Navy Seal style inflatable was christened "Big Black," and it very quickly became an all-important link to safety, sanity, and salvation. Built from a heavily rubberized PVC material, these boats are all but indestructible and, in our case, would soon be put through just about every test imaginable. She was powered by a fifty-horsepower engine so there was always power to spare, with plenty of room for crew and gear. Big Black was too big for the boat deck, so whenever we'd head offshore, the crew would deflate her, then hoist her to the boat deck. Otherwise she'd be towed behind us, always within easy reach for a quick shore reconnaissance or as a backup life raft were our real raft not to inflate.

After leaving Halifax enroute to St. Anthony's, we dropped anchor in North Arm Harbor, a stunning and secluded spot in The Bay of Islands. While Dominique, Sefton, Clinton, and Ulli climbed into Big Black to explore, I remained aboard to pay some bills, send emails to help pay those bills, and make needed calls. I also needed to care for my Toe From Hell, which had started to explode again. The pain starts as though someone was trying to cut the incision with a hot knife and gets worse from there. In the past, rest and elevation seemed to help and, with everyone off the boat, I hoped to do just that.

Up anchoring and heading north again, June 30 rolled into a beautiful night with wall-to-wall stars. We'd worked our way far enough north so that the sun set around 9:45 p.m. and rose again around 3:30 a.m., never experiencing total darkness.

Outside on the deck, the air was almost cold, a small reminder of the fact that we were inexorably making our way up to the Arctic. The only sound apart from the low, distant rumble of *Bagan*'s engine, was the hissing as her bow cut through the dark cold ocean water. Knowing that all good things will come to an end, I tried to revel in the moment of purpose and pure solitude. The connection with nature and all she can offer was immediate. With none of the day-to-day distractions of land-based life, one's senses heighten, and what normally would pass unnoticed, now commands more attention. It was after perhaps twenty minutes of this I felt a small, almost imperceptible change.

This difference was also evident all around me on deck; tiny drops of moisture cast soft reflections of our green and red running lights. A fog was quickly moving in and, judging by the moisture-laden air now brushing against my face, it was going to be a heavy one. I went back inside the pilot-house, made sure both radars were tuned to their best limits. So sensitive were these units, we could actually pick up birds in fight. The Automatic Identification System (AIS) was up and running, depth indicators and electronic charts running as they should be. Nothing to do but make a mug of tea, sit back, watch the instruments and, on a regular basis, go outside on deck to try and get a good feel for where we were.

As we rolled into the next day and the sun was illuminating the fog around us, Dominique saw an extremely large target that wasn't moving, especially out of our way. The persistent, heavy fog that had settled in around 2 a.m. gave an ethereal feel to a light not quite twilight or dawn. Yet what was now showing up on the radar four miles to the north was so large neither fog nor low light could hide it; our first official sighting of an iceberg was an amazingly impressive one in that this berg had to have been at least a thousand feet long and more than 100 feet high. The fog was playing tricks in that first this "thing" was there, then it wasn't. When I could see it, my immediate impression of the massive hulk in the fog was that of an aircraft carrier. It had to be, nothing was that big and tall and actually moved.

As there wasn't sufficient light to photograph it, Dominique and I went through every possibility we could so that we could define it for the others as they revolved into the watch schedule; there were no rectangular, steep-sided islands charted for the area and it was too irregular to be any sort of cargo ship. Looking at it through the glasses, we could see the jagged and rough outline it presented against the northern sky. There was no doubting that it was truly a mountain of ice. And, as the minutes ticked by, our sighting was confirmed by the presence of several others—albeit not half as large— mini-islands of ice. By now all were up and crammed into the pilothouse, all with cameras in hand and soft exclamations about the size and power of these giants. The first sighting of ice is one that I will never forget. It's no exaggeration when I realized that the icebergs held power, strength, drive, and a presence that could truly not care less about who you are or where it is you want to go. They travel along silently. Seas break against their frozen and rock-hard surfaces, exploding with furious impotence as this massive structure of blue-brown-white ice keeps its determined course. Yet, as we were to learn, their presence wasn't always known. A few hours later, I'd rotated out of watch and was below cleaning up when I heard Dominique say from the pilothouse, "Jesus, that one didn't even show up on radar."

It was hard to ignore such a comment so I went up to join her and immediately saw that we were now in the company of many more of these floating, silent icy sentinels and, sure enough, a particularly large one about three miles off our bows failed to register even as much as a blip on the radars. Yet some smaller ones, perhaps the size of Volkswagen Beetles, stood out bright and conspicuous on the green electronic screens.

All through that foggy morning, as many sets of eyes that were available were glued to either one of the two radars as ice targets and bearings were called out to the helmsman of the hour.

No exaggeration to say there were five sets of nerves on a knife edge. As the hours ticked by and the heat of the morning sun started to cook off some of the fog, we became more accustomed to the ice and a bit emboldened. I asked Clinton to take us closer to a particularly large iceberg that had amazing shapes, ledges, tiny waterfalls, and brilliant deep, ice-blue colors glowing from within. Very capably and with great precision, Clinton all but drifted *Bagan* up to this massive berg.

On the grand scale of things, it was far from massive but when you're in a boat one-tenth its size, it fit the definition of "massive."

Sefton and Dominique scampered out to the bow with cameras followed by Ulli with one of the HD cameras. Clinton and I remained in the pilothouse. He and I were talking about the "power" this thing gave out when, from the foredeck, I heard Ulli's voice in no uncertain terms, "Move, get the hell out of my shot, you're in my shot!!" Life was back with a vengeance. My stomach curled up into its all-too-familiar knot and my heart sank. It seemed as though Sefton had inadvertently walked across Ulli's sightlines as he was shooting the iceberg. Sefton should have had his eyes open and Ulli should have laughed it off. They worked it out but I was left with a feeling that an apparent lack of respect was starting to develop aboard, an insidious attitude that could greatly affect the trip. I chalked it up to the excitement of it all and moved on. Clinton continued edging closer to the berg and when we got perhaps fifty yards away, felt that that was close enough and started to back *Bagan* down. For this part of the trip, we were towing Big Black along behind us and as Clinton put it into reverse I realized that there was no one on the stern assuring that we didn't back down over her or at least the line attaching her to *Bagan*'s stern.

I ran through the pilothouse, looked off the stern, and saw that the line was sinking below *Bagan*'s stern, slowly heading to the prop with Big Black following close behind. I hollered up to Clinton to put *Bagan* in neutral, "Now!" I learned quickly that Clinton did not like being given orders with a "now" attached. "I know what I'm doing," he hollered back.

I let it go, and apologized for my quick comment, though I had genuine concerns about safety. A few minutes later, I was trying to distract myself and was washing the morning dishes. Ulli came up to me with the camera and asked what the commotion on the stern was all about. I tried to explain as dispassionately as I could that it was a miscommunication and that we all learned from it. From the pilothouse rang Clinton's voice, "I can't believe you're still going on with that shit."

The morning's incidents brought up something I needed to deal with within myself: with more than 120 days ahead of us, when was the appropriate time for issues and comments to be addressed and when were they to be ignored and forgotten about? For the past few days, with the tension of the fog and ice, comments were tossed about impersonally, but I started to feel a growing angst from Clinton and Ulli both. At one point, Ulli ran out onto the deck to get a great shot of birds gliding by one of the many ice palaces we saw. He failed to shut the door behind him. From his helm chair, Clinton loudly reminded him to "Shut the fucking door," and went on to add to all within earshot, "I hate that fucking guy." Do I address this and, if so, publicly? Is it worth pulling him off the helm, or anyone for that matter, and immediately address the issue? Or do I wait until that right time and try to share my feelings? Do I get specific or give a general character summation and share what I expect and not expect from all of us on the trip? Before we left Newport, I tried to have a few talks of this nature but knew at the time there was no frame of reference for those whom I was talking to as that was then and now is now.

Around 4 p.m. that afternoon, we came across two remarkably shaped icebergs not 100 yards from each other. I asked Clinton to slowly take us up to them as they presented some amazing filming opportunities. Again he deftly maneuvered *Bagan* into position and at no faster than perhaps a knot, steered *Bagan* between the two for Ulli and the rest of us with still cameras. I don't know which I heard first but very quickly learned that where we were heading wasn't such a great idea. The depth alarm started to squawk and from inside the pilothouse I could hear Dominique on the bow yelling, "Back up, back up!!!" Seems that the two bergs were actually one and they were connected by a 100-yard-long shelf just three feet under the water. I was prepared for the ensuing crunch and was doing a quick mental inventory of what was up in the bow and wondering just how thick the fiberglass around the bulb at the front of *Bagan* was. Amazingly, there was no crunch, no grinding to a sudden stop. *Bagan* quickly slowed, stopped, and slowly began to back up. A silence fell over *Bagan* and then sheepish smiles started to form. No one said anything other than, "That could have sucked." And once again we headed back to course and onto St. Anthony's not daring any more intentional close encounters with ice. That was the first lesson with ice shelves, a lesson that wouldn't come into play until more than three months later, but one with as deadly a set of consequences as anything we had encountered to date.

The next day, July 1st, with a heavy fog allowing us no more than fifty feet visibility at any given time, we felt our way along the coast and what our eyes couldn't tell us, the two radars, three GPSs, and electronic charts did; we were right on course for the entrance to St. Anthony's, the "Iceberg Capital" of the world. Slowly, we powered towards the opening to the harbor that still only the electronics were showing us. The radar indicated that the entrance was now perhaps fifty yards off our bow but all that our eyes could see was the continued dark gray wall of fog. Peeping in and out of it to the left was a rock-faced wall with the ocean's swells breaking upon it. The wind was less than five knots but the power of the sea could not only be seen but also heard.

Clinton was steady on the helm and while I was confident in his every move, I was perhaps ten seconds away from suggesting that we bail out of the approach, head back out, and either wait for a break in the fog or more of an indication. He simply pressed on, aiming for the opening that we saw on the charts and radar. A few seconds later, we broke through the well-defined wall of North Atlantic fog. It didn't simply dissipate or "lift" as one second it was there, the next not. We were right on course and exactly where all the instruments and charts told us we were. If anything, the fog gives birth to and coddles second-guessing and I was still trying to get around mine. Greatly relieved, I turned to Clinton and said, "And that's why I hired you; the best of the best. You've got cajones of steel, sir!"

As we worked our way through a small commercial fleet toward our anchorage, St. Anthony's proved to be what we'd been told it was: beautiful, colorful, small, green, and welcoming. A brilliant midday sun illuminated deeply vegetated and rocky hills but for once without the usual collection of tall evergreens. In the past few days, we seemed to have traveled close to or above the tree line. Hoping to find a good weather window to make the 800-mile passage across to Greenland, we planned to stay in St. Anthony's just long enough to download some weather charts. We knew that there'd be plenty more ice out there, but it'd be nice to shake some of the fog and make actual visual contact instead of that on the radar.

There was no way of knowing at the time that "just long enough" was actually "too long."

CHAPTER 5

WEATHERING THE STORM

Once we were secured away at the head of the deep, calm bay and with anchor down and firmly set, we took to Big Black and powered the half-mile into the small town of St. Anthony's, tying up at the town dock.

By now we all needed time to stretch, reconnect with our land legs, and, of course, try to find the closest internet connection. While St. Anthony's is no small town—it boasts a population either side of 2,500—I was surprised at how empty its streets were, perhaps an indication that although called the "Ice Berg, Whale & Bear Capital of The World," it isn't a town overrun with tourists scrambling to get a glimpse of any one of the three. Small local businesses, fishing co-ops, and chain retail stores lined either side of its small, winding Main Street. St. Anthony's gives the impression of a "hard working" town surrounded with lush green hills, scattered with modest one- and two-story homes, and as we were to find out, filled with good and honest people.

Situated on the northern tip of Newfoundland, St. Anthony's sits on the west side of "Ice Berg Alley," a name we weren't all that anxious to learn more about but that has seen more than its share of ice-related tragedy over the years, including the story of a small fishing boat quickly crushed and sent to the bottom. This alley is where all the small to large ship-killing icebergs slowly and inexorably float down from the Greenland Ice Sheet at the head of Baffin Bay and wend their way out into the North Atlantic, sometimes not completely melting for several months and thousands of miles. Most certainly this area was the birthplace of the iceberg that ultimately sank the Titanic in 1912.

Once ashore, our first stop was at the public library where internet connections finally were made, emails answered, and weather charts studied in closer detail. Inside the main cinderblock entrance—and not wasted on any of us—stood a reminder of what lay ahead. Encased in glass was a stuffed polar bear that easily stood ten feet at the shoulder and, although long dead, it still carried mention of the massively powerful and ultimate predator that he once was. A while back, this emboldened guy made his way into town one day. Thankfully no shots were fired and ultimately he was chased out by helicopter. Unfortunately the chase was a bit too much for him and he died of a heart attack.

Once upstairs and into the library, we all soon found the only available area to sit was at the Lilliputian-sized children's desks scattered throughout the room. Sitting in basically doll chairs, balancing laptops on wobbly tables supported on knees covered with foul weather gear, we tried to catch up with that which we left behind only a few weeks earlier. The five of us pounding away at our laptops making the occasional mumbled comment proved a sight as odd as any, which most certainly gave pause to those folks who wandered in and out of the library for the next few hours. It was also here that Clinton started to download the Canadian Government ice charts to study the one element that could end this trip in a heartbeat: unpredicted ice.

Due to the constant and somewhat unpredicted flow of icebergs north to south in Baffin Bay, crossing over to Greenland was going to be like trying to cross a busy highway; the timing had to be perfect. So respected were these bergs that the oil companies hire "Berg Cowboys" who use their monstrous and powerful tug boats to slowly tow the ice skyscrapers onto a different course so that they'd pose no threat or danger to the companies' off-shore oil and gas platforms.

What particularly grabbed Clinton's immediate attention was a developing low-pressure system that held the potential to keep us in place for several days. The crossing to Greenland would be dicey as it was, so I had no problem with waiting for a weather window to allow us to scoot across the 900 or so miles to Greenland's west coast and then follow that north to Nuk (or as it's sometimes spelled, Nuuk), the capital city where we'd clear into the country.

As we were leaving the library and heading off in various directions to explore or do some more last-minute provisioning, Clinton made a curious comment that helped illuminate my feelings of great concern that had started to come to life only days earlier. Under gray and threatening skies, we were heading back to the town dock where Big Black was tied up, waiting, gently bumping up along the wooden docks as the cool and dampening breeze started to fill. "It's started, it looks like a shit storm," Clinton offered. That certainly caught my attention immediately. I asked him to elaborate. "The Bering Sea ... it's blowing a full gale there now and will be for a few more days, " he said. I was a bit curious, as the Bering Sea was at least 2,000 miles and two months away. Having no real concept of just what he was talking about and why, I didn't know if I wanted to encourage his thoughts by asking him more about what he saw on the charts. I did know that I couldn't afford to get pulled down into his deep concern. It would be months before we got to the Bering Sea, if we got to the Bering Sea, and these gales would blow themselves out in days if not hours.

I simply couldn't—and now found that I refused to—make the connection. Clinton is the best weather guy I've ever worked with. His forecasts and intuitions about what a given low or high pressure may do and how it will affect us in days to come is second to none. Sometimes his forecasts bordered on the brilliantly uncanny. But his concerns eluded me. To get us off the subject of a gale that had zero bearing on where we were now, I asked him about his immediate weather concerns. He didn't let me down in that he had "diagnosed" the pending low sitting on top of us and had already formulated Plans B, C, and D in the event it grew in intensity.

It did.

For the next few dreary, wet, and gray days, we sat on the hook in St. Anthony's and waited for a weather window that would allow us to cross the needed 900 miles to Greenland. The three components we watched for were fog, ice, and wind—all of which could be found and interpreted from weather charts that we could download from the internet. If it were raining too hard—which it did non-stop for five days—we could use the ship's computer to try to catch a stray signal from shore, if the computer behaved properly. We also could hook into a satellite and access the Web. Or, if we felt up to getting wet, we could hike back the half-mile through town and once again try to squeeze ourselves under the tiny desks at the library. The decision to cross to Greenland was a bit of a witches' brew. The wind from the northwest would tend to dissipate the fog but also drive more ice down from the Greenland Ice Sheets in the north, filling Baffin Bay and south with perhaps thousands of bergs of every possible size. In many ways, these massive ice monuments defy all logic in that even the radar had issues with them. There are times when the radar would pick up a piece the size of a small chair and in the same sweep would miss one as big as a house.

On the other hand, if the wind blew from the southwest, it would clear the crossing and safely drive a great deal of the ice to shore but also bring in fog. We had to consider whether we wanted to be in large ice fields that we could at least see or be locked in fog with less ice that doesn't become evident until we're right up on it.

The other dilemma was the wind.

Do we sneak out of there on the back of an increasingly large high-pressure system to take advantage of diminishing breezes? If we did, would the usual low pressure develop right behind it and give us more wind and seas than we bargained for? Again, in either case, as we further studied the charts, we saw there seemed to be a component developing on the west side of Greenland that promised to deliver thirty-knot winds out of the north, against a knot-and-a-half north-setting current, which equals our old friend "chop"—big, steep, closely spaced seas which would make for a brutal crossing.

According to the latest weather charts, the new plan would be to leave early the morning of July 4 and try to make the dash across and through the ice; a dash that we hopefully wouldn't be celebrating with any unplanned bangs or booms. The morning of July 3 I awoke to the now familiar sound of rain pounding on the decks. The building wind outside was blasting our hull and *Bagan* was "sailing" at her anchor as she was pushed this way and the other, "sailing on the hook." The low still hadn't moved on, and once more, after consulting the latest weather chart, we saw that we'd be stuck aboard *Bagan* yet a few more days.

At one point that morning, I stumbled up from my cabin to the galley to make tea and ran into Ulli sitting with Sefton, giving him valuable but perhaps not truly needed lessons on the inner workings of one of the cameras. Ulli was being his usual thorough and professional self but Sefton was clearly elsewhere, throwing the occasional sideways glance in my direction. After a few minutes of this tutorial, Sefton excused himself under the pretext of needing to go below. As he passed me sipping my tea, he quietly said: "He's starting to get on my nerves, Dad," and walked on.

As the rain-driven morning rolled on into a bit of a clearing in the afternoon, we came up with a plan to go ashore. Dominique wanted to go to the supermarket and top off once more. Not knowing what we were or weren't going to find in the way of food inside The Passage, she wanted to take advantage of every opportunity that she found. Ulli also expressed an interest in filming her going about her shopping which I too felt would be a good scene in the documentary.

My plan was to stay aboard and catch up on the blogs for the website. It was also about this time that again, the Toe From Hell started to screech. As before, it felt as though a white-hot scalpel was cutting from the top of my baby toe up about an inch into my foot. I couldn't figure out what in particular was aggravating it, but felt walking a few miles wasn't going to help matters. I went below to grab some aspirin as well as my credit card for

Dominique when I heard the beginning of an argument between Dominique and Sefton in the salon over a baseball cap and it was escalating quickly. Sefton was wearing the cap in a shot meant to focus on Dominique, and she felt it was inappropriate for the filming. Occasionally, I heard Ulli's voice chiming in. I don't know if it was the parent in me, the stressed-out owner, or simply my poor judgment but in I went, trying to settle an issue that in hindsight wasn't an issue at all, certainly not one in which I needed to be involved.

All went off to town a bit in a huff. I went below to write, in more than a bit of a huff myself. After I cooled off, I decided that when they came back, a discussion was in order to tell them I was wrong for sticking my nose into the problem. I also wanted to hear if the cap issue resolved itself on shore.

We all met in the pilothouse where I apologized. Yet it was during this meeting that a new issue emerged, an issue that once again had my stomach in that familiar grip of cold granite and stress. Dominique was the first to bring it up; concern and respect. She felt as though we had started to become a bit sloppy in our respect levels for one another. As she was talking, it was becoming apparent that the focus of her concern wasn't directed as much on any of us as it was Clinton. Bravely she said that she was tired of the names and abusive language that Clinton had been calling her and she had reached her peak. Very eloquently, she said in the past few weeks it had become intolerable. She was brave and forthright in her choice of words and how she delivered them, never out-and-out accusing but saying that "This is how it feels to me." I was extremely proud of her for baring her soul and hurt in front of us all, something that's extremely difficult with just one other person, let alone a full boat's crew. I was also extremely saddened to see that her concerns for the most part fell on deaf ears and were countered with threats that someone would have to leave, or that she needed thicker skin. Nothing moved forward from that. Sefton and I tried offering that communications between Dominique and Clinton were affecting all of us and suggested ideas to help such as more meetings, private or full crew. They both had the onerous task of not only getting *Bagan* where very few other boats had ever traveled but also trying to maintain their five-year relationship in plain sight of all.

Nothing but tears came from the discussion, with Clinton and Dominique simply agreeing to disagree. After that, the tension seemed to decrease. Dominique's airing of the problem in an honest and non-threatening and mature way gave her great relief from which we all benefited.

It wasn't to last. I felt at the time that Clinton, like me, needed time to digest and work through issues. But quickly after the pilothouse talk, he distanced himself and was uncommunicative, an attitude that I hoped was going to simply blow by. A few days of waiting for the low-pressure system to either fall apart or roll over us had grown to five or potentially eight. We were restless and edgy. *Bagan* was starting to develop a bit of a funk in the air, the funk of five people living in tight quarters. The funk of a locker room came to mind. Quarters were growing tighter and despite us all trying to keep positive spirits, the delay did begin to take a toll. At one point, Dominique had the unenviable task of telling the rest of us to pick up after ourselves and do our dishes. Eventually she devised a wonderful "cleaning calendar" which, on a weekly basis, rotated each of us into and out of cleaning, dish washing, and vacuuming. Later in the trip, with a few cagey bets, these various jobs could be foisted off on another, such as handling the dreaded dish washing for the day. Regardless how well we were handling things, the pressures of being cooped up on a fifty-seven–foot boat on an anchor continued to mount. Slight tension was once again building in the air. I declared July 4 an official day off, and offered a rental car if someone wanted to get as far away from the water as possible. I also said no filming and that no one had to wear Ulli's dreaded wireless mics.

Shortly after my announcement, Ulli quickly said he wanted to film and mics were definitely going to be needed. My patience with Ulli's relentless professionalism was growing thinner. Ulli was a pro, one of the best in the business. But by this point in the trip, it seemed as though he wasn't quite able to judge whether requests would be received well or when they'd blow up in his face. His focus was the filming and that took first priority over anything, day off or not. Ulli was adamant and after thinking about it, I didn't see the harm in asking the crew to take the few minutes to clip their mics on. I also stressed that the day's filming was to be of the crew taking a day off... no set ups, no posing, no nothing. It was their day off. He completely agreed.

The quick off-again on-again edicts prompted some justified grumbling. I found my stomach turning to cold granite as I heard an excessively loud and pointed grumbling coming from Dominique and Clinton's cabin, grumblings that I felt were being said for my benefit. I was tired of unwarranted grumblings and snide comments and felt as though this was another instance of the messenger being shot. I'd reached my limit. Dilemmas like this are often found in the everyday world, but the difference was in that world you were in a space perhaps 100 times larger than where the five of us now were. In the "normal" world, at the end of the day you could go home and try to leave it all behind. With our tight living quarters, anchor watches, and shared cabins and bathrooms, there was no "end of the day" for any of us.

Clinton needed to know in no uncertain terms my feelings about his attitude. Through a closed door, I said that I'd made a mistake, and suggested that he suck it up and roll with it. He continued to complain, and within seconds I found myself offering that I was beyond tired of his "letting off steam." In the meantime, I suggested, he was to "wear the fucking mic."

That was the very last place I wanted to go. Despite how I'd tried to rid myself of them, all the pressures of the past year had grown to untold proportions. We were not a quarter into the trip and seemingly wherever I looked, there was a new and growing and debilitating problem. As I look back at it, my now choosing to go head-to-head with Clinton was surely tipping the scale towards a dangerous area.

While the others took the day off, I chose to stay aboard, to write, think, and honor my screeching toe. Someone had to stay and watch the boat as the wind was still pretty steep, and while *Bagan* carried a 175-pound anchor, there was always a chance she could drag. Dominique, Sefton, Ulli, and Clinton did indeed rent a car and went exploring while I managed to fill the day while doing some deep soul-searching.

Shortly after all were back aboard, I called a meeting to share what I'd been debating, my conclusions and my concerns. I wanted them to know that they all had a voice in the conclusions I'd come to and in this instance by no means was my word the final word, but they needed to know where I was. I told them I couldn't be happier with their work and focus but that there was a growing attitude aboard I could no longer ignore. I told Clinton that as far as I felt, he was the best-of-the-best but that I was fed up with his arrogance, second-guessing, and attitude. If things didn't improve immediately, I said, I was giving serious thought to calling off the trip and heading back to Newport. We were already at a stress level that I didn't think we'd reach until we were well into The Passage, I said, adding that I was tired of walking on eggshells.

Also, as the organizer and major (only) backer, I felt there would be times when I had to stick to my guns. I didn't enjoy the position I was in, but I did know that for my sanity, we needed a change. It didn't go down well. Clinton stood and said, "I'm not going to listen to this shit on my day off." He asked permission to take Big Black ashore and simply left. We all sat in silence. I immediately felt that either I hit the nail on the head or had grossly misjudged the situation aboard and had just single-handedly killed the future of the trip.

Dominique was the first to speak. She was devastated and in tears. "You threw him under the bus." She was very upset for the trip as well as for Clinton and needed a release. I tried to point out to her that I didn't say anything to him that she didn't say the day before. Sefton offered very quietly: "Look, we're going to do The Passage, we just need to adjust."

Dominique was still in tears, worried where Clinton might go, what he might do, or if he was coming back. It was then that I learned that in their five years of being together, it seemed that he'd had a history of simply disappearing when things got tough for him. For the next hour, I truly didn't know if once the low pressure passed, we'd be heading north or south, if we'd be five or four. I had to come to peace within myself that if we turned back it was the right call and that if we continued north that too would be the right call. I knew that right or wrong, whatever I decided, I couldn't back away from it.

A few hours passed in relative silence. The rain was lightening up and it was my fervent wish that moods would as well. We all heard the gentle bump of Big Black against *Bagan*'s hull. Clinton came back aboard, looked me square in the eye, and said, "You're right . . . I've been a little Hitler." Clinton apologized.

He also told me something that was remarkably candid and forthright. He noted that I was a sponge; that I'd taken all these hits—financial, weather, crew, and health-related—and I had not let out anger or disappointment. He said he'd watched as I'd contain them, hoping to shield everyone else from my emotions. He was right; I tried to absorb the hits and not have the crew worry about things. It was a fine balance for me because I didn't want to ever show anything other than concern for them and their jobs. I felt that if I shared with them every single time the trip took a large enough hit that made its future an immediate challenge, it may take away from their enthusiasm. No time for fear, worry, or panic.

To this day, I maintain that in my position, I needed to show consistency and the ability to deal with what was thrown at me—or us as a unit—and to know the difference. Clinton was right; it was impossible for one person to keep an even keel after all I had to deal with in the past eighteen months.

But right or wrong, this was the way I felt I must proceed. I agreed with Clinton and told him that it was a precarious position, this leader stuff, and that in the future I'd try to do better.

There was another wonderful moment that day. At one point, I went below to my cabin and literally bumped into Dominique coming out of hers. She stopped me and said she was sorry not to have tried to help me more with Clinton and that she had more to learn from me about communication. On the surface, this was a wonderful compliment. Yet, as a "daughter to a stepfather" moment, it was one of the most golden times that I can recall. The bumps and bruises that our broken family had taken in the past were now slowly fading and it was then that Dominique—this wonderful, beautiful young woman whom I'd first met when she was five—and I took a giant, loving step forward in our child/parent relationship.

July 4 couldn't have come at a better time. That night Dominique cooked us an amazingly "American" dinner (sloppy Joes, French fries, a big, fresh salad) and the boat was festooned in red, white, and blue.

Later the next afternoon, I saw that the water tank was fairly low so I went down to the engine room to turn on the water maker—a system that uses high pressure pumps and multiple filters to extract the salt and impurities from sea water, delivering approximately forty gallons of fresh water an hour.

Several hours after I turned it on, I noticed that the gauge on the water meter in the pilothouse hadn't budged, indicating that the tanks hadn't received any water. After checking hoses, pressures, and filters, I called Clinton down into the engine room. He arrived with schematics in hand and together we tried to diagnose the situation as best we could. We found that a malfunctioning solenoid had sent eighty gallons of fresh water back in the sea.

That cold, granite feeling in my stomach was back. I was quickly going through my supply of Prilosec. Clinton was remarkable at reading schematics and diagnosing problems but after a few hours of doing what he could, came up with no answer. Our new budget-busting $14,000 Sea Recovery Aqua Whisper Water Maker had crapped out after less than twenty hours. Calls were placed to the installer but to no avail for after a half hour on the phone with him, running diagnostic tests that we'd already run, we quickly learned it was a factory problem and not his.

If we couldn't fix the problem with the water maker, the trip to the Northwest Passage would be over then and there.

CHAPTER 6

THE CAMERA DOESN'T LIE

What started out as yet another misty and cold morning with temperatures in the mid 40s in St. Anthony's harbor, quickly turned into one of the most memorable days of our entire trip.

I was sitting in the pilothouse, writing and trying to coax every ounce of sunshine out of a day identical to the previous eight, which all had been equally dreary. The weather charts showed movement of a hoped-for high pressure system which, in theory, would move the persistent low out of the area and give us a few days of easy and dry northwest breezes. That was the scenario we were fantasizing, one that was slowly becoming a fantastical sailor's yarn.

Mother Nature has only one agenda and that is hers alone. What the charts and prognostications show couldn't be of less interest to her and her mysterious ways. I was wrestling with the satellite hookup, which, over the past few days, had slowly started to become problematic, when Clinton sat down in the pilothouse seat next to me. These black, leatherette seats were fully supportive in that they had adjustable backs, height adjustments, and a small shelf on which you could set your feet. They were designed and built to keep you in place during extreme weather. Without looking up from my writing, I greeted him with the usual, "What's up?" His answer: "I found a work-around for the water maker." To say I was elated and stunned was a pure understatement.

"There seems to be a manual diversion valve which isn't really explained in the books. Once we're making good clean water, we flip the switch, it overrides the solenoid and diverts the fresh water into the tank."

Within seconds, Clinton and I were both down in the engine room where he proceeded to share the results of his sleuthing. Hidden away in the back of the unit was a button. This discovery was part-and-parcel of why I hired Clinton. When he was "on" there was no touching him. He could size up a mechanical situation and find several solutions while I was still trying to get my arms around the original problem. The discovery of this small button meant that the success of the trip was once again a viable option.

At the time, neither he nor I knew if this would be a completely work-able solution or merely a temporary fix. But until that time came, I had to assume all was back to normal, for now.

Clinton and I once again assumed our positions in the pilothouse in front of the computer screens and once again downloaded the latest weather chart. This particular download was excruciatingly slow but what we saw looked extremely promising.

"We are outta here!" was how Clinton chose to let the others know. There was a flurry of arrivals in the pilothouse and soon all five of us were staring at the hot-off-the-satellite weather chart. The high we'd been hoping for had developed and was quickly moving the low out. The wave height chart showed a substantial decrease in the height of the seas and wind charts showed the breeze laying down. The long-awaited weather window had formed. For the four-day crossing, we'd have two days of flat seas with the potential for the breeze and seas to fill in for the last two days.

Sefton looked at the chart, smiled, then opened the door to the pilot-house to go out and ready the foredeck for our departure. "It's been real St. Anthony's ... it's been fun ... but it's not been real fun." Before the trip began, I'd assigned crew their various jobs. Dominique as first mate would run the galley and "domestics" side of the boat. Clinton as captain was responsible for navigation and was head engineer. I'd seen Sefton gather and absorb more and more experience through the years and, on the basis of this, assigned him the foredeck and coordinating all landings and departures.

Because of her sheer size, Big Black didn't completely fit on the boat deck and her engine, which weighed in excess of 150 pounds, had to be removed and stored below. She had to then be partially deflated and hoisted up to the boat deck, a laborious process which took upwards of an hour.

We set our departure time for 4 p.m. and, after jobs to prepare for this four-day offshore leg were attended to—securing of parts in the engine room, books all back in the racks, food stores dug out of the storage areas, hatches bolted, pertinent charts organized—we all waited to hear that wonderful sound of *Bagan*'s 325-horsepower engine coming to life.

Clinton was behind the wheel, Sefton and Dominique on the foredeck, and at the appointed time and after eight days in St. Anthony's, the anchor once again saw fresh air and we were again on our way to the Northwest Passage.

The weather chart was right in that for the first few days, we were in flat seas and with very little breeze. Making her way across Baffin Bay and over to the west coast of Greenland, *Bagan* simply hissed, glided through the water at eight knots, 192 miles a day. We all stood easy watches and slept soundly as previous tensions seemed to have magically vanished.

Happily, I felt as though we were all again back on the same page.

Now that we were finally making progress in the right direction, the stresses of the trip had taken their proper place and all seemed manageable. The weather was sunny and for that area of the world, warm.

Settling into the mid-fifties, the sun bathed us in a warmth and dryness we hadn't felt in more than a week.

Without the stresses of weather or close living, we all felt unburdened and freed up to enjoy and reflect on just what it was that we were setting out to do in the next four months. I watched as Sefton and Dominique spent more off-watch time together, talking, listening, and, most important, laughing, which so wonderfully showed that these two did indeed have a loving and caring history together. Their ease, joy, and humor with one another was created years ago. Life is never 100 percent and all siblings have their moments, but it was apparent that these two had shared a supporting and loving life.

As I watched, I was aware this was a double-edged sword. I felt so blessed to be a part of these two—but now I couldn't help but reflect on that which over the years I'd missed; from the iconic learning to ride a bike to that moment when their first love didn't work out. It is endlessly tempting to reflect on the moments in their lives for which I wasn't present and sidle up to self-recrimination and remorse.

That's an easy route that I've always felt serves no one. But, ultimately, such angst has to help us reach a peaceful place. Yet it was in these very self-reflective moments when I'd start to think that the events that happened in our family were events which would hurt and guide the three children—Chauncey, Dominique, and Sefton—in the wrong direction. For me, this sort of thinking always held the potential of spiraling into a false and dangerous area. I needed to look at what had occurred, accept it, and try to manage what I had now, in the best way for all. What had been lacking before was in wonderful evidence now as the two "children" I now saw in front of me were laughing, poking, and sitting quietly. Our trip to The Passage that had begun as an abstract dream and adventure, had slowly become a family event that held potential for a closeness and discovery that very few parents would be lucky enough to experience.

It was bliss.

Soon Chauncey and Greg would be joining us. I had no idea how Chauncey would fit into the scenario I was now watching before me, how and if family dynamics would change, if he would feel this growing sense of family or simply be another great, but non-attached, crew member.

Chauncey is an entirely different character and, as such, brings an entirely different set of experiences and hopes. It was going to be an interesting dynamic of which to be a part. By the same token, Greg coming into this family unit was of special concern because he wasn't family and was going to be an outsider. Greg is a man of few words and strong feelings. I hoped he'd fit in smoothly.

My moments of reflection were brought back into the present-day reality. "I'd like to do an oil check." Clinton pointed out that since we'd been under power for a few days and while all engine temperatures were in the "normal" range, it would be a good idea to see if we were burning oil. Because this check was an important part of life aboard *Bagan*, I felt it best to get at least a few of these moments down on tape so I alerted Ulli to get a camera ready and we'd mic up. This time, adding the microphone was met with approval and enthusiasm. To check the oil, we'd need to throttle back and shut down the main engine. The seas were glass-flat and this was the perfect time to get an accurate measure of the oil reservoir without slamming back and forth across the hot engine room. After about five minutes of preparing and letting everyone aboard know we'd be shutting down, Clinton throttled back and then completely shut down the engine. As we both headed down to the engine room, there was no mistaking the agitation in Ulli's voice: "Too soon... Not now... Damn it, I'm not ready!"

He very strongly asked us to start again, which was something neither Clinton nor I was willing to do. Clinton was clearly irritated, as was I, at the urgency and adamancy of Ulli's request and his answer was simple and direct: "Fuck off... I'm running a boat, not making a fucking movie!" Not the exact words I would have chosen, but definitely the very same intent. There'd be other oil checks and for now Ulli would simply have to shoot what he could. My feeling to this day is some shots always will be missed amid the vagaries of a journey such as this. And if one has to create or recreate a scenario in editing, then so be it. This is a time-honored production argument but it was a situation where I felt I had to stand firm and simply say: "It is what it is. Next time."

The oil checked out as hoped and shortly we were on our way across Baffin Bay to Greenland. I went down to my cabin to write when Ulli appeared in my doorway and said we needed to talk. I wasn't surprised. He was very upset about our not waiting for him to set up. The ship came first, I said, adding that I'd hoped that he could capture the full process the next time. Ulli listened, nodded, and replied that no one was helping him with the project, no one was logging tapes, working with the cameras, and wearing their mics at all times. He said he was already tired of Clinton's constant blow-back and that I wasn't helping him enough to create shots.

Everyone had specific jobs, I told him, and if they could help in other areas they would. I hired Ulli for all the filming needs, period. My argument didn't seem to hit his mark and he continued to vent. Ulli wasn't looking for an answer as much as he must have been feeling the tension of the past few weeks and needed a release.

I felt it was my job to listen, and Ulli needed a sympathetic ear. I promised I would speak with everyone and remind them he needed their help.

At that point, I could have used someone to vent to myself.

As Ulli left my cabin and headed up the small stairway to the pilot-house, I could hear Clinton coming down. I let out a sigh. But instead of a complaint about this morning, he apologized to Ulli as they passed, "Sorry about this morning. I was wrong and should have given you more time."

That was about as good as it gets.

As the ocean ran under *Bagan*'s keel, we noticed that the expected breeze was filling in from the south-southeast and building, producing long fat swells that *Bagan,* so far, handled in stride. The air was becoming heavier and thicker, and dew droplets were starting to form on the stainless steel safety rails that bordered *Bagan*'s decks, suggesting that fog was on the way. A fresh chart quickly showed us that the expected system had grown and was going to arrive more forcefully than previously thought. As Clinton had predicted, the last few days of the crossing were going to be bumpy, and from all appearances, it looked as though it'd be starting that evening. At this, "evening" redefined itself. We were now starting to experience 24-hour light and while the sun did briefly dip below the horizon, night—in the normal sense—never truly did fall. In its place was an eerie, bluish tint that was cast upon everything about us. At "sunset," the light switched from the normal daylight to a cast blue and white, leaving faces with slight gaunt and hollow appearances. I worked my way up to the pilothouse to the salon for a much-needed mug of hot tea.

Walking aft I slid open the stern door and went out onto deck. The thick, cold fog had settled in around us and we were once again in a gray and damp void where all sounds and breezes seemed to defy logic.

Standing there, sipping my tea and reflecting on where it was the trip now stood, I realized that the area we were now powering through was as historic as any because for hundreds of years, man had passed through this area of Baffin Bay to find new discoveries and report back on what they encountered.

Perhaps no tale is more curious than the story of the *HMS Resolute*.

In April 1852, under the command of Edward Belcher, the *HMS Resolute* and four other ships left England to search for the lost Franklin Expedition. After two years of fruitless searching, and finally frozen into the ice, Belcher ordered the abandonment of the *Resolute*. The men took to the ice, hiked out to safety, and returned home to England on *HMS North Star* and the relief ships *HMS Phoenix* and *HMS Talbot*.

The abandoned *Resolute* continued to move slowly eastward in the pack ice, and in September 1855, almost 1,200 miles away from where she had been abandoned, a whaler from New London, Connecticut, saw the *Resolute*, now basically a ghost ship adrift in the pack ice in the Davis Strait. He split his crew and sailed her back to New London. When word of her arrival in Connecticut was announced, Congress approved $40,000 to refurbish her and sail her back to Britain. In 1856, she was presented to Queen Victoria as a gift. Years later, after the *Resolute* was broken up, Queen Victoria asked that several desks be built from her timbers, one of which was presented to President Rutherford B. Hayes in November 1880. Since 1961, the *Resolute* desk has sat proudly in the Oval Office of The White House in Washington.

Despite ironic stories from maritime history, as the cold further surrounded me, I realized that we were now entering the same waters that through the years had swallowed so many ships and crews.

Leaving the cold, damp air behind, I made my way back inside *Bagan* for some much-needed warmth. "Shrimp Creole and I've no idea how it's going to turn out," Dominique said with a laugh. The aroma of Dominique's cooking preceded her announcement for the night's dinner and from what I now smelled, it was going to turn out wonderfully. Nothing cheers up a boat faster or more thoroughly than a long-cooked, hearty meal and Dominique was now elbow-deep into preparing ours.

"A 'sparement'?" I asked, referring to the "experimental" meals she cooked as a seven-year-old child. Hands down, Dominique has the best laugh I've ever heard. It's a combination of grown woman, beer hall, and small child. It was with this great laugh that she threw her head back and asked, "Oh God... Do you remember that?" I thought back to the many "sparements" which were all presented with a child's great care and love. Dominique's dinner was a great success and gave us all needed nourishment.

As predicted, the next morning weather brought about a less-than-subtle change. Breezes were now clipping past thirty knots and the seas were in excess of eight feet. *Bagan* took it all in stride but rolling, and slamming; conditions which warranted needing two hands to get from here to there. In sloppy weather, something as simple as brushing your teeth requires bracing with your free hand, sometimes your knees, just to stay at the sink. Other activities in the head need the dexterity and balance of a circus performer.

Despite the bouncing, *Bagan* kept on true course and on July 13 in a clearing breeze, we powered into Nuk's busy commercial harbor and started the hunt for dock space. Surrounding this harbor were steep, rocky outcrops, void of vegetation but peppered with colorful houses. Here we needed to clear the whole crew officially into Greenland, catch our breath, and take on needed fuel for a next leg that would hopefully see us up and into The Passage.

We circled the harbor and docks looking for even the slightest opening in the commercial congestion; workboats in all sizes were stacked up three and four deep along the harbor walls and floats. Realizing we wouldn't find a spot by ourselves, Clinton gently moved us alongside of a 100-foot, heavily rusted and oil-soaked barge-like vessel rafted up against two well-worn fishing boats in excess of seventy feet. Not the best situation.

We managed *Bagan* into position, secured her lines, and after four long days at sea, shut down the engine. Before we could go on shore and explore, ship's duties called: engine room checks, log entries, a thorough cleanup, and blankets and sleeping bags aired. I took time to write blogs for later uploading and tried to finish the few articles I was writing about the trip.

What struck me more than anything was that we were now in Greenland, a place and destination that had previously occupied a spot only in my mind's eye, not reality.

Yet here we were, where many previous expeditions had staged their final stop before attempting "The Passage." It wasn't lost on me that their survival rate was not good. Once we dropped the lines from Nuk and headed north, the rules of the game were going to change drastically. There were no time-honored methods of approaching The Passage. Cruising guides, channel markers, or simply word of mouth hardly existed. The leg that would find us maneuvering our way north through Davis Straight, brought us to seldom-used anchorages and waters so cold they would kill in minutes anyone unfortunate enough to fall overboard. The colorful dream had become a black-and-white reality.

There were still several days to prepare for this next leg as well as tend to all of *Bagan*'s needs. Our immediate goal was to find and clear Customs, then find a good restaurant and take the crew out to a relaxed dinner that Dominique didn't have to prepare. The clearing-in part was easy. Any cop can do it we were told. However, in three days we never saw a cop or for that matter a meter maid.

Dinner was a bit more challenging. I had little cash and at meal's end the bill came to a staggering $450. All things considered, I'd rather have been back offshore rolling side to side in heavy fog.

Yet, the pain of this dinner bill paled in comparison to the 1,500 gallons of diesel we were soon to try to take on.

CHAPTER 7

BLACK MOODS IN GREENLAND

"I**t is still not going through, just enter your PIN."

"I did. Let me try another card."

We'd managed to put 1,500 gallons of diesel into *Bagan* with little trouble, but paying for it now was turning into an unwanted international saga.

After two days in Nuk, looking for nautical charts of the immediate area, replenishing food stores, and downloading weather charts, we found that a nice and fat high pressure system had moved in and was starting to dominate the area. It was time to leave. All we needed was to refuel, then start the next leg up the coast of Greenland.

The weather charts showed we were going to be having winds less than ten knots and flat seas for the next week, so I thought it best to take advantage of this improved weather window and start working our way up Greenland's west coast before we made the cross over the top of Baffin Bay and on into Lancaster Sound—entrance to the Northwest Passage.

All of us were ready to get back to sea. I was particularly anxious to reach Sisimiut, our next big stop where we'd be dropping Ulli off and picking up Chauncey and Greg. By now, each crew member had told me that while they appreciated that Ulli was a dedicated professional, they had had their fill of the constant filming demands. I'd come to the point where I felt the ever-present tension aboard, whether large or small, could be lessened if we didn't have the "constant camera" syndrome. Even I found myself running out of patience and support for Ulli's constant needs. Not being well-versed on how to dissipate the relentlessly building tensions on a fifty-seven-foot boat, I hadn't much to draw from, so I was hoping Ulli's departure would lessen the growing pressures.

Soon we would be taking on two new crew members. They would be involved in the everyday workings of the trip, and I had high hopes about the change. We'd come a long way since the baring of souls in St. Anthony's but something still didn't feel right. There was a constant underlying tension that, while not palpable, continued to bode ill.

I am prone to falling victim to those inner voices that wonder and project, perhaps trying to make something of a situation that doesn't really exist. Many times in my life, these feelings have stood me well. But given the small space we were all now sharing, I realized that physical proximity could automatically bring extra angst.

As we got farther from home waters and closer to the entrance to The Passage, the gravity of what we were undertaking was playing more on my waking and sleeping time. More than any trip or experience I had ever undertaken, I knew that if things went wrong for us in the next few months they could do so with deadly results.

We'd brought *Bagan* into the gas dock across Nuk's busy commercial harbor an hour earlier and once secured at their floating dock—which had an unmarked, Volkswagen-sized rock not two feet under the water at its east end—started taking on the 1,500 gallons which would see us deep into The Passage to Cambridge Bay.

This fuel would run the main engine at a burn rate of approximately six gallons an hour and supply the backup engine, the generator, and the much-needed diesel heater.

"You need a PIN to complete the purchase. Why is it you Americans don't have PINs for your credit cards?" Up to this point, the attendant at the fuel dock couldn't have been more helpful or accommodating. Now his attitude was going south about as fast as my belief that this was all going to end well. Through my foreign travels, I've found that when the words "you" and "Americans" are placed in the same sentence, it's not an encouraging sign.

To complete the fuel purchase, I needed to enter a PIN in the credit card machine. After calls to American Express and MasterCard revealed they don't issue PINs, each suggested that I could write a letter.

Assuring the attendant that all was well, I went back to our boat and told all within earshot that we had to pool all the cash we could find. We had $2,000 aboard for "ship money" but needed a couple of hundred more than that. After everyone rummaged through pockets, we managed to come up with it. Crisis averted. For now, anyway.

Anchor up and with *Bagan* a few tons heavier due to the new fuel, we headed out the next morning through the entrance we had used two days earlier and started north up the mountainous, barren but beautiful west side of Greenland.

Seas were flat and winds light and variable. Clinton was at the helm, relatively speaking, since *Bagan* also had two autopilots that could steer a more precise course than we could. We always had one of the autopilots engaged while the other served as a backup. The autopilots were indispensable and using them was a simple matter of entering the ship's intended course, which we got from our electronic chart system which itself gathered information from one of three GPSs.

Yet we took this simple combination one step further in that we had the GPSs and the autopilots all talking to the ship's computer at once. In a micro-second, that would give the autopilot feedback to adjust to the course we set into the electronic charts.

I decided to take advantage of the wonderful weather and hooked my MacBook up to the computer through our onboard wireless network and started to upload some new pictures to the website. Once connected, I watched the megabytes tick by as the photos traveled the approximate 50,000 round-trip miles into and back from space onto our web site. As in the past, all went smoothly until I received a message on my screen that I was to fight with for the rest of the trip: "Connection Lost." This being the first time I'd received that message, it did little to dampen my enthusiasm for this amazing feat of technical wonder so I happily shut everything down and tried again. And again, "Connection Lost."

With satellites and Iridium being one of the world's most powerful and advanced telecommunications companies, the current problem was obviously a technical glitch on our end, so Clinton and I checked programs and tried once again.

Two megabytes short of full upload, we got the same message: "Connection Lost." Again and again and again. By this time in my life, I'd learned enough about computers and myself that I knew it was time to calmly step away—albeit totally vexed and irritated—and try to distract myself with other jobs. Later in the evening, if we could get a satellite phone connection, I'd try contacting web page designer, Matt Dutra, to see if he could call Telaurus, the vendor who provided the connection with Iridium, and see if they could check things out on their end. I was paying $1,000 a month for this satellite interface and felt I clearly wasn't getting my money's worth. Whether successfully or not, I tried to keep my immediate concern at bay as by no means would it be the end of the world if we couldn't upload the pictures and blogs but it would mean we no longer had the direct means to let friends, family, and a growing list of followers see how far we'd gotten and what we'd encountered. It also meant that there was nothing to show the badly needed potential sponsors.

The next night, at 10:41 p.m. and in full daylight, we ghosted into and dropped anchor in Sondre Stromfjord, one of Greenland's deepest fjords that runs more than 100 miles deep into the vast and mountainous interior. After tending to a few ship's duties—running the generator for the reluctant water maker, switching over to the ship's inverters to power our 110AC needs, and rotating some of the freshly bought food from refrigerator to crock pot—we fell into our anchor watch schedule, which allowed me six hours of sleep.

I awoke from a deep sleep and for the first time in quite a while found *Bagan* to be completely motionless, utterly silent. It was perhaps three in the morning yet light was pouring through my cabin hatch as though it were midday. Somewhat awake, I went up to the salon to grab my usual middle of the night snack and take a moment for another gaze at our icy paradise.

Instead, I saw a sight of higher curiosity. Where Sefton normally would be found sleeping, on either of the two settees, he wasn't. Both settees were empty. I went up the few steps to the pilothouse and slid open the hatch to the boat deck where in the past few weeks he'd been known to snooze and sleep through the night. No Sefton. I went below to check the other two cabins. Curiosity was quickly moving to a special zone of panic. The idyllic beauty that our remote location offered moments ago was now conjuring up far-less-than-pleasant scenarios. A quick look showed that he wasn't in Ulli's small, two bunk crew-cabin.

Opening the door to Clinton and Dominique's forward cabin, I saw a sight that further confounded me; only Dominique was to be found in her queen-sized bunk. She was sound asleep. I jiggled her toe. She slowly started to wake up and before her eyes were even close to wide open I threw at her, "Where's Sefton... Clinton... did they take Big Black?" Fully awake and alert now, she said she had no idea where they or the inflatable had gone.

We both went back up to the salon and checked for a note. Nothing. I saw that all two-way radios were in their charging racks. The guns were still aboard. Their total lack of communication and inadequate preparation for their field trip was a situation about as grave as we'd faced to date and my parental concern was now spilling over into anger at their lack of thinking and respect for not only the trip and the rest of the crew but for the potential threats that surrounded us. We weren't quite yet in polar bear territory but polar bears didn't have exclusive rights on killing. I was still tired, exhausted from all the problems the trip had met with up to now, and for one of the few times in my life, I think I chose the correct and healthy route. I told Dominique that there was no point in us both waiting for them so we might as well head back to bed. "Oh no... I'm waiting for them, don't worry about that!" Knowing full well that when they got back, Dominique would most certainly express her feelings about their ill-prepared departure, I flopped back into my bunk and fell immediately back to sleep, only to be woken in less than an hour by Ulli getting up and knocking about, grumbling about the dry heat in the boat, opening and shutting lockers and talking to no one in particular about the camera gear.

Further sleep wasn't in the cards, so I now got up for the day and made my way up and aft into the salon just as Clinton and Sefton were arriving. I tried to make it short and sweet: "If you want to explore on land that's fine. The fact that you didn't leave a note, take guns, or two-ways is inexcusable. This will not happen again." Sefton understood, was apologetic, and judged the timing before he told me of the otherworldly beauty they saw. Clinton offered up, "We're not kids and knew what we were doing."

I chose not to engage them. I felt that we'd all need the strengths and support of each other and that, at this point, I couldn't afford to alienate but at the same time, I needed to express my reactions if I felt them to be valid enough.

Over breakfast, Sefton and Clinton told us about the remarkable beauty and solitude they encountered ashore, and we agreed that a hike to some of Greenland's most beautiful offerings was in order. We packed into Big Black and set off for hours of exploration if not badly needed "alone time." On our way in, Ulli was getting video of the ice-blue water and remarkable visibility when he asked Clinton to slow the boat down in a sharper-than-normal tone. Clinton goosed the fifty-horsepower throttle a tad and made Big Black lurch forward a few feet. The sudden movement threw Ulli off balance. He glared at Clinton angrily. "Don't you look at me like that," Clinton shouted, ending all communication between the two then and there. The tension was ratcheted up another notch.

Securing Big Black, we all took to the shore to find ourselves surrounded by low lying scruff and berry patches, stunted by harsh winter winds. Runoff from faraway glaciers scoured paths through ragged and powerful rock outcroppings bordered by thick, wet moss and dense green shrubbery.

Various deposits of animal waste let us know that we weren't alone in our exploration, yet we saw none. As we climbed the small rock faces and slowly strolled the small open spaces that resembled a Tyrolean meadow, I found myself unwinding and releasing the worries of the trip, increasing the feelings I had felt on deck the night before. The air was slowly coming alive with different layers of scent. The strong freezing winds that buffeted us were nuanced, layered.

Through the open areas of low bramble and damp ground, I looked back at *Bagan*, now a tiny speck anchored securely in the midst of steep, snow-covered mountains that appeared to press down from all sides. I thought back through all the history that I'd read about the many attempts to transit The Passage, the parties going in vain search of the lost Franklin Expedition, the whalers who plied these waters for centuries. I felt our efforts had moved us into a realm of the few who managed to get this far north. Where we now stood, where *Bagan* was anchored pumped new enthusiasm and drive into me.

I looked down the small ravine and saw Ulli trekking his way up to meet me. I walked down to help him with his load and was immediately greeted with "Where's Sefton? He's supposed to be helping me!" Being slightly pulled from my revelry of the past few moments, I told him I'd no idea where Sefton was and didn't know about any arrangement which they'd made. "Well he obviously doesn't take this trip or film seriously!" was Ulli's sharp and pointed answer.

I blew back at Ulli, telling him I was sick of dealing with attitude and went off to find a small corner in the side of the rocky hill to lay back, think, and sunbathe, depleted not by the expected mechanical malfunctions but by the unexpected and heated confrontations and how I was to deal with them.

Prior to departure from Newport, I had tried to think about all the things I could imagine that would go wrong and came up with many Plan Bs. Never did I think about crew attitude or counterproductive remarks that could easily chip away at the focus and excitement of the trip.

The sniping we'd all been dealing with since Halifax was taking a toll. From my perch high above the small cove where *Bagan* was anchored, I watched Big Black shuttle people back and forth. Feeling that I'd stewed enough, I stood to start the short hike back down the small, rocky ridge. After my first step, I quickly sat back down. It felt as though a pack of hornets or perhaps a snake had worked its way into my boot. The sharp cutting pain ran from my toe up along the side of my foot—the white-hot pain of my Toe From Hell. I sat and waited as it ran its shockwave through my foot. By this time, I found there really wasn't anything I could do for the pain. It was a returning infection I had to be concerned about.

Waiting for the ache to subside, I pulled off my boot and sock and was relieved to see that my toe looked pink and healthy. But I would have been more relieved had I found that snake or hornet.

When I got back aboard, I sat down with Ulli in the pilothouse and I told him I was cutting short his time aboard *Bagan*. The tension was sapping my energy just as the hard part of the trip was arriving. Ulli took it in stride. He is a great human whom I remain proud to call a friend.

Clinton later told me that he and Dominique had heard my "conversation" with Ulli up on the hill. Clinton said Dominique had been upset by the tone of our conversation, and said she would "Set Ulli's ass straight!" When I heard this, I beamed inside for Dominique's concern.

On July 17, we crossed over the Arctic Circle. Watching on the electronic charts as we did so found me simply shaking my head.

There simply were no words for my elation.

I looked outside the ports at water rolling past *Bagan*'s hull and saw and felt the miracle of the trip unfolding. We were quickly closing in on a place few had been before. The survival stakes, although still low, were mounting every day.

Two days later, we arrived in Sisimiut, our final stop before crossing Baffin Bay to attempt The Passage. To date, we'd encountered no truly serious weather and all systems were more or less behaving. After many dropped and frustrating satellite phone calls, I had finally arranged Ulli's flight out. Soon Chauncey and Greg would be coming aboard and we could hopefully concentrate on the next leg without distraction.

Although Ulli's departure was bittersweet, it did give everyone a chance to breathe and relax.

The on-time arrival of Chauncey and Greg brought hope, a tonic that would be fully concentrated on the 4,000 miles and extreme unknowns ahead.

By the time they flew in, we had moved *Bagan* from the inner dock area of Sisimiut's commercial harbor and into the deep bay a mile to the north. While at the docks, regardless of how clean we tried to keep *Bagan*'s topsides, each morning they were covered with commercial soot, seagull crap, and the occasional half-eaten fish. Out in the bay, internet access via satellite was more of a direct shot, which allowed me chances—futile—at uploading pictures.

Clinton kept an eye on the weather downloads, saw that the area was under its usually high pressure influence, and we picked the departure date in two days, July 24—forty-eight hours to get groceries and nautical charts plus allow Sefton, Chauncey, and Greg hiking time. While the hills and mountains surrounding Sisimiut weren't the snow-capped offerings we saw a few days earlier in Stromfjord, they did present steep-sided faces that rose perhaps 2,000 feet above the town.

Once settled in the outside bay, the first morning I awoke at the usual time, made my usual black tea, and tucked myself away up on the boat deck to try to gather thoughts and feelings that were by this time running the full gauntlet of sublime to ridiculous. Trying to keep the issues and concern from getting ahead of me was now an official job. Nothing would truly be resolved until the end of the trip, whatever form that may come in.

After we had all grabbed our breakfast and gathered in *Bagan*'s salon to plan the day, Greg, Chauncey, and Sefton started packing for the day's hiking while Dominique and I readied Big Black to take her to shore. Although it was just past noon, Clinton was still in bed.

Successfully making a beach landing on a rocky and not particularly welcoming shore, Dominique and I dropped the others for their hike and we motored back to *Bagan*. Unexpectedly, Dominique throttled back, put the engine in neutral, looked at me with her steady eyes, and said, "I think you'd better talk with Clinton about last night and Big Black."

Dominique was loathe to blow the whistle on Clinton and most of the salient facts I had to pull from her, but floating there, in Big Black, in the middle of one of Greenland's more beautiful bays I listened as the words, "8:00 a.m.," "drunk," "fell in the water," "locals," "fight," and my all-time favorite, "police" were said.

It appears as though Clinton closed a few bars, couldn't find Big Black, got into a shoving match with some locals, fell in the frigid Arctic water, and at one point met the police (Clinton was later to say all of it, except losing Big Black and falling in drunk, was a joke that he was trying to pull on Dominique). We sat in silence. I was sick. My heart was being wrung out, my stomach on fire, my throat starting to close. I couldn't speak. Over thirty years ago, when I stopped drinking, I found myself not being comfortable around those who still drank. In the company of drunks, as I such was, I became intolerant. I tried to understand this attitude of mine and not pass judgment.

Once again, the future and success of the trip was at hand, by this time it was smack dab in my face. As I watched a cruise ship leave Sisimiut's inner harbor and head out to sea, I so wanted to be aboard that ship, leave *Bagan* to the crew, throw a maxed-out credit card and some money in their direction, and simply say, "Call me if you make it."

Dominique and I sat in silence. Both of us were on the verge of tears. She for having to tell me a very hard truth, I because my dream and focus for the past two years just took a large enough hit to be classified as a death blow. I so wanted to share father-daughter moments with Dominique, explore new areas within ourselves, emotions of the past which I suspected could lead to current-day and powerful connections.

There was no hard-fought decision; what I then battled with was black and white. This time I wasn't going to seek the crew's feedback, this decision was mine and mine alone; depending on how the rest of the day went, what conclusions I came to, who owned up to what, the next morning I found again that *Bagan* and crew were going to be heading either north or south, with or without a captain.

CHAPTER 8

FAREWELL, CIVILIZATION

Welcoming Chauncey and Greg on board was one of the more surreal and uplifting moments of the trip. Seeing Greg, my dive partner from Rhode Island, now in Greenland and aboard *Bagan*, was proof that despite the momentary setbacks, the trip was indeed heading in a positive direction. And witnessing my stepson Chauncey aboard, this young man, whom I first met when he was eight, was a moment that swirled about in my memory, generating excitement, sadness, happiness, hope, and promise.

After all these years, simply having the chance to sit down with Chauncey and reconnect would have been a gift; now we were going to be able to do this while also attempting to transit an area very few before have ever managed to do. With Chauncey, Greg, and Sefton off hiking and after learning of the bad news from the night before, Dominique and I landed Big Black back at *Bagan* and set about getting her ready for a departure I hoped would soon get us all away from Sisimiut and the complications it brought.

With a mug of black tea, I planted myself back in the familiar seat in the pilothouse, in front of the computer, writing and hoping for a successful upload. There'd been no word from Clinton, who, I was assured, was below and sleeping. From time to time, the stale smell of cheap booze would waft up into the rest of the boat, an odor that brought back ugly memories.

With fingers crossed, I was watching as the last of four photographs were successfully uploaded to the website when, from below, Clinton stumbled into the pilothouse, groggy and "left over" from the night before. He smiled, asked what was new, and was basically trying to grab his bearings. There was no discussion, no questions nor explanations of the previous night's hijinks. By this point, I had lost a lot of confidence in Clinton not only as a friend but also as a hired captain. I felt a heart-to-heart talk would be pointless.

"You left us without Big Black. If we had an emergency, we'd have been stuck while you were drunk and unaccounted for. That shit will never happen again. End of discussion." The unfortunate part was that at this point of the trip, I needed Clinton and his full cooperation. I could easily find another competent captain or take over the running of *Bagan* myself, but Clinton had put almost a year into the effort and trying to bring anyone else up to speed would have been all but impossible. Clinton's answer was simple and direct, "Copy."

I didn't expect contrition, but right about then a flicker of responsibility would have done wonders. He went below to the galley to grab some food and found a waiting Dominique. Her comment and feelings about the previous night were every bit as brief as mine and to the point: "You're a total asshole." To which Clinton immediately rose up in defense. I went topside to the deck, as I simply couldn't listen to any more. This was a problem that wasn't going to simply go away on its own. I'd learned from Dominique that the behavior wasn't anything new and why I hadn't seen it for the several years of knowing Clinton before the trip was due to careful and judicious planning.

Later that afternoon, the shore party signaled a pick up and, when back aboard, filled us in on the sights, heights, and mosquitoes that they'd encountered. Earlier, I'd gone on a brief shore walk and as with Chauncey, Sefton, and Greg, found these flying hypodermic needles to come in swarms that seemingly could not only block out the sun but were fully capable of carrying off a small dog if not the side of your face. We plugged in one of the HD cameras they had taken with them into the ship's flat screen and what I saw was exhilarating and wildly encouraging; Chauncey and Sefton had managed to shoot some beautiful footage of the surrounding area.

I wanted them to capture the trip as they saw it, with some guidance from me, and with 400 hours of blank tape, they could afford to shoot whatever and whenever they thought it worthwhile. It was a remarkable and completely unexpected moment, to turn the filming over to these two.

Chauncey and Sefton had the benefit of spending many years together after the divorce, growing up in the same conditions under the same roof. For reasons I'll never quite know but fully appreciate, Chauncey and I slowly grew apart, a separation that I believe was based in hurt and disappointment. Simple facts had it that I wasn't around to see this artistic side of Chauncey come to life and grow, but, as with Sefton, here it was in plain evidence and there was no limit of parental pride and love to see it all in full display. As with Dominique and Sefton, I knew there was no way of undoing this past pain, so I hoped that this new and unexpected role of his was a means by which Chauncey and I could reestablish, find a mutual bond, and build from there.

Watching the footage of the day's hiking on the flat screen was showing me a possibility, a means by which he and I could start the growth back together. I was extremely moved by his and Sefton's filming talents but more moved by the fact that after fifteen years, Chauncey and I may have started in on a road back to forgiveness, understanding, and love.

Another unexpected surprise at this time was the immediate acceptance of Greg. One of my fears was that as the family unit reassembled and started to redefine itself, it would be difficult for Greg, a relative stranger to all but me, to find his way into this crowd. Prior to departure from Rhode Island and in Greg's absence, I had informal talks with everyone alerting them to the potential of Greg feeling as an outsider and not working his way in, or more to the point, not being allowed to work his way in. Over the years we'd learned a lot about each other, how we both ticked, how we reacted to stressful situations.

I'd come to learn that Greg was a consummate pro in all things boating, diving, and photography, but as such he was a man of determination and may not always voice his immediate concerns. My fear was that there was potential for him not to feel like a solid part of the team as much as that of a "hired gun."

But Greg's integration into the already established crew and new family was seamless. That day, which started off far less than good, was wrapping itself up on a note of encouragement and great hopes, for, as we watched the latest weather chart come in off the internet, we saw that what was a large high that had been over us for a few days now had grown larger and deeper; blue skies and flat seas would be in evidence for at least the next five days and once again we found that the time to go was now.

On July 24, in a bit less than ten knots of air and with some sloppy seas still in evidence, we left Sisimiut's outer harbor bound for Disko Bay and then due west, across the top of Baffin Bay and into Lancaster Sound, just south of Devon Island. From an Inuit guide, I had been advised a year earlier that I shouldn't attempt a transit of The Passage until at least the end of July, so while we were more or less on schedule, we did have a few days to burn as the crossing wasn't going to take more than two or three days. Our plan was to slowly work our way up the coast and, if all indications were good, once again make a dash across iceberg packed waters and into The Passage, or as it would later feel, into the "Looking Glass."

The weather charts were right about the breeze but off a tad about the state of the seas. What were supposed to be a bit lumpy seas were more like a washing machine and they quickly took their toll; Dominique wasn't in a great rush to make any meals as none of us were in much of a rush to eat. Juice and crackers seemed to be the order of the day and, as *Bagan* twisted, turned, and dipped with each lumpy leftover sea, a few crew were seen hanging over the downwind rails outside on deck. Not quite an auspicious start to our next leg.

Aasiaat is a small fishing community which, as with those we'd seen before, plays host to a handful of commercial fishing boats as well as a small assortment of private, recreational boats. Feeling that this would produce a great place to stop for twelve hours in a pea soup fog, we threaded our way into and through a small outcropping of islets that were not much more than rock and moss. The entrance required the utmost in concentration on the wheel as the deep channel which ran between the rocky outcroppings was narrow and precisely defined.

The bottom was every bit as much rock as were the islands we wove between and what made this particularly challenging was that due to the choking fog, we had to do it all by depth gauge and radar. The pilothouse was as silent as it'd ever been and the tension and fear that we were all experiencing was, which is odd to say, the right sort of tension and fear, based on the safety and success of our efforts. The fog that had grabbed us not a day earlier still surrounded us and only afforded slight but building visibility as we came into Aasiaat's outer harbor.

After a day of rest and a good night's sleep in this small fishing community, we headed back out into Baffin Bay to continue working our way north to Disko Island. As hoped, the fog had dissipated and the seas flattened out. Our getting underway marked the beginning of a two-day stretch that up to that point in my boating career, were the most remarkable of my 40,000 miles at sea.

What was going to be another one-day hop up the coast to the next anchorage quickly turned into one of maneuvering between massive, blue-white icebergs hundreds of feet high and perhaps twice as long. These powerful yet slowly moving concentrations of thousand-year-old ice held caves, tunnels, hollows, and coursing fresh water melt that were more steam than trickle. With each subtle movement, whether they were grounded or not, great creaks, groans, and rumblings came from far deep inside of them. Imperceptibly shifting, making their way from Greenland's Ice Sheet towards the open Atlantic in the south, they were the epitome of silence, stealth, and grace. They were slow-moving, wondrously beautiful, silent killers.

Were we to get too close at the wrong time, 600 feet and untold tons of ice could roll on top of us, pulverizing all fifty-seven feet of *Bagan* into the frozen bottom of the sea. Yet it needn't have taken such a large and dramatic event to have us simply disappear; were a large part of any one of these massive icebergs to break apart, the tidal wave this could create could potentially roll us. Trying to gain the best route through these was a constantly slow maneuvering with very precise and deliberate actions; no bow wave, no sudden and loud blast from the engine as this noise could trigger them into action. Even though they weren't tightly packed and at most times allowed perhaps fifty or more yards between them, it felt like a limitless maze in which one could easily become hopelessly seduced.

With one eye set to find our way alongside and through them, the other was constantly looking back at where we'd just been, as an escape route was always a needed comfort.

To bring this remarkable display of nature to a head, we found we had fallen in with a small pod of humpback whales that took absolutely no notice of us. Lolling on the surface with great and lazy flapping and slapping of their flukes and tails on the still, silent, and deep blue water, they too worked their way through and past these great towers of ice. After only minutes into this ice field, we started to ready Big Black for some needed video and stills. No sooner had we powered into the company of these whales then I saw that Big Black was now in the water with full film crew aboard in record time. Despite the low, slow droning of the fifty-horsepower outboard, these leviathans still seemed oblivious, regarding us perhaps as a horse would a gnat.

As powerful and awe inspiring as this otherworldly ice field was, it was all too easy to remember that, regardless of the side of the cause on which you fell, the numbers of bergs we were dealing with were increasing yearly as global warming was breaking up the Greenland Ice Sheet faster than predicted. Disko Bay and the ice sheet function as a barometer for global warming. I didn't come armed with facts to prove or disprove this, but being in the middle of what was clear evidence of an increase in summer temperatures was as sobering an experience as they come. We were among firsthand evidence, not sterile numbers. Satellite pictures have proved iceberg totals are increasing and the "melt" is lasting longer every year. To be at Ground

Zero for these observations was a direct and demanding experience that mesmerized us.

At 2 p.m., we pulled ourselves away from the Arctic beauty we'd been a part of since early that morning to continue on our route outside of Disko Island, across Baffin Bay and into Lancaster Sound. While we were no longer in the packed concentration of these bergs, we never quite lost touch with them. Clinton and I were on watch when we saw a very peculiar shape coming up over the western horizon ahead.

As we worked our way closer, it was proving to be the largest iceberg yet. Perhaps 500-feet high and 800-feet wide, its top like an alpine mountain, complete with sharp and pointed peak, it was a sight that, judging by the silence of the now-gathered crew, was the most unique of the day, until we came along side of it.

In the upper third of its 500 feet was a perfect "O," a circle through which one could have flown a small plane. Chauncey, Greg, and Sefton jumped into Big Black to get footage and stills of *Bagan* next to this remarkable ice formation while Clinton, Dominique, and I stayed aboard to get footage of them getting footage. No one spoke as we tried to absorb it all.

With the sound of a cannon shot, at the very top of the "O," a piece of ice perhaps twenty feet by fifty feet simply let go and did a free fall for what seemed like twenty seconds before it landed flat on the water below. The explosive echo of its landing reverberated around us, boomeranging off other icebergs and the sea itself. Immediately, Big Black scooted over to the base of this berg to try to perhaps capture video of more falling ice. To this day, I look at the footage and I remain astonished by the scale; Big Black being nothing more than the smallest of black dots against a jagged, white, blue, and gray floating mountain.

With far more self-discipline that I'd ever had to exercise, we pulled ourselves away from the icebergs and continued up the coast heading along the west side of Disko Island, and settled into a small and protected anchorage for the evening with hope of a fresh start across to Lancaster Sound in the morning. It was at this approximate latitude that the doomed Franklin

Expedition was last seen. When they crossed from Greenland to the entrance of The Passage, they decided to try to sit out some weather and secured themselves to the lee side of an iceberg.

We dropped the hook in a remote, deep, and barren anchorage on Disko Island's west coast called "Norde Laksebugt." As we slowly circled through the open anchorage, looking for good depth and holding ground, I was outside on deck trying to take in everything, attempting to absorb and process all I could see and feel. The land was now stripped of all obvious vegetation and the brown, jagged hills had taken on a very unwelcoming tone.

The wind was raw, dry, and cutting. Whether it has been storms in excess of seventy knots or gentle zephyrs, deep down I seemed to always know, or at least respect, the unseen forces with which I was dealing. But this wind was alien, no comfort to be found, only cold strength and potential threat. Bit by bit, the familiarities and constants of all I had become used to on the water were changing, growing more threatening and tinged with the surreal.

With anchor firmly set, we started the familiar drill of getting ready for a night on the hook and aiming for an early start the next morning. What one normally associated with late fall or early winter—steam from the galley starting to build up on *Bagan*'s windows—brought a much-needed sense of comfort. Dominique had started cooking a crock-pot meal of chicken, vegetables, and rice while Sefton and Chauncey began to drag their snowboarding gear from the engine room.

Their enthusiasm was contagious and while Big Black was shortly heading to shore with all but Dominique, who knew alone time when she saw it, Greg, Clinton, and I chose to wander and explore the length of the gray, windswept, rocky beach.

Leaning into the cold Arctic blasts, I headed out down the beach by myself, turning every few moments to monitor their progress toward the small snowfield. Despite the frigid blasts, I beamed with pride and excitement for the two. They were both passionate about their sport and as they made their way up the side of the mountain, their excitement could be seen in their body language. Yet far deeper than their passion, I felt that I could see the love and ease they had with each other—two brothers with a deep and long relationship. Perhaps it was nothing more than parental pride and overthinking but I could "feel" more than actually hear their laughter.

Yet, nothing is singular in its offering, and from this a new and unfamiliar feeling was slowly forming inside of me as I watched the two brothers. "Are they going to be okay?"

They were pros who were both well-versed with backcountry hiking, had all but grown up on snowboards, were the type to take calculated risks, carried two-way radios to communicate with the boat, and this time took rifles. Yet here I was mentally hovering over these two grown men as though they were walking across the street for the first time by themselves. By this time, I'd wandered down the rocky beach perhaps a mile, taking the chance to walk into and through the low bordering Arctic shrubbery for a few hundred yards. Thick and woven into tight bunches, the vegetation would at times be dry, almost as loose as desert tumbleweed while at other times it would be hiding a shallow bog that from time to time would appear to have on its surface the slightest of oil sheens, a rainbow of colors which none too subtly reminded me of the attention the Arctic area had recently fallen under. We were now at the edge of what many countries were examining with more scrutiny, an area that is not only known for its pockets of natural gas and oil, but its vast amount of precious minerals as well.

Looking out at the miles of emptiness and natural beauty, it seemed inconceivable there was potential that this could be the leading edge of what might be explored, that there may be a time in the not-too-distant future that what I was now observing would change for the worse. I've come too far in life not to realize that profit trumps promises and, as we were to continue deeper and deeper into the Arctic, I saw firsthand just how much more would be at stake.

Once back aboard and after another of Dominique's dinners, Sefton and Chauncey hooked a playback camera into the flat screen and showed us the efforts of their hiking and snowboarding. I was stunned by the lengths they went to film their boarding. Wide shots, medium shots, tight shots, walkthroughs, POVs, low angle and high, they had covered every aspect of the hike up to the small snowfield I was more than pleased—I was astonished.

Both Sefton and Chauncey have great eyes and natural artistic gifts that were in complete evidence by what I was now watching. A huge and pressing responsibility had further been lifted from me, and by the end of the viewing, I had offered them the complete control of the filming for the trip.

As I settled into my bunk that evening, I was again able to feel the original sense of challenge of what lay before us.

The experience in and among the ice and whales, with not so much as another boat or person in sight, brought home the feeling that we were heading into an area and transit that very few had ever done successfully. Yet framing that excitement was the feeling that anchored in that small cove, I experienced far more isolation than I'd ever felt before.

After consulting a 3 a.m. weather and ice chart, both Clinton and I felt that although still early, it was time to cross. A benign weather window had opened and we had to grab it while we could. High winds and steep seas weren't anything we wanted to try and cope with for the crossing to Lancaster Sound as all it'd take would be for *Bagan* to slam off the back of a steep sea onto a half-submerged piece of ice on the other side and we could potentially severely damage the hull or any exposed parts such as the prop.

Our original entrance to The Passage was to start at Pond Inlet, just south of Lancaster Sound, but as the ice charts showed us that this opening was still choked, we felt it best to add an extra day and head farther north. A calculated risk. We'd never be entirely free of the icebergs on our more northern crossing.

Early that next morning, we set our course for the 80th meridian just inside Lancaster Sound. Depending on the source of your reading, the "official" entrance and exit to The Passage varies. Ours was just west of Baffin Bay and south of Devon Island. It was still a few days off and for all intents the weather was going to hold for several days after our entrance. History was starting to slowly close in around us. This area was the last staging point for Captain Francis Leopold McClintock who, in July of 1857, set off from Disko Bay aboard his fully crewed 132-foot ship *Fox* in search of the lost Franklin Expedition.

While McClintock and company never did find Franklin's ships or the missing men, they did come across bones on King William Island that exhibited signs of cannibalism. Once back in the U.K. where he reported his findings, McClintock was met with anger, outrage, and extreme disfavor. He and his findings were publicly ridiculed as Victorian England apparently was not willing to hear that one of their national heroes, John Franklin, would have resorted to the depravity of cannibalism to assure survival.

Leaving Disko Bay behind and crossing to the west toward the opening of The Passage, life aboard *Bagan* continued in the same vein as it had for the past few weeks, with an underlying air of anticipation and excitement. Long periods of silence were broken by moments of lightness as any one of the six aboard would try to dodge the weight and gravity of what was soon to be upon us. We were heading into an area of the Arctic where the exit rate was way out of proportion with that of the entrance rate.

About a day out from the entrance, we found ourselves in need of a distraction, and "flew" Sefton out over the water with Big Black's hydraulic davit. Greg rigged a climbing harness rig for Sefton that allowed him to be raised, lowered, and extended out over the water for "off-boat" shots of *Bagan* as she moved through the water at eight knots.

For the next twenty-four hours, we rotated in and out of our watches, all eyes on the electronic charts as we inched closer to our entrance mark into The Passage. Dominique spent the morning baking the Official Entrance Cake, Chauncey filmed, I slept, albeit fitfully, Greg read, and Clinton ran the boat. We were all scattered across *Bagan*'s fifty-seven feet, settled into our own small and immediate worlds, when we were thrown onto the same page with the same dread and concern.

The sound from the engine room was far from that of the usual engine rumblings and the steady rhythm I'd been listening to since the day I bought

Bagan five years earlier; it was irregular, loud, and extremely wrong. Without exchanging a word, Clinton bolted below to the engine, I replaced him on watch, and everyone stopped and stared at the door to the engine room. The news was not good.

A pump for the hydraulic system that powered the stabilizers and the bow thruster had seemingly blown a gasket and lost a lot of the packing grease that kept the bearings cool and spinning freely. For close to two hours, Clinton broke down the system, repacked it with grease, and did as much of an overhaul on the small pump as possible. While the demise of this pump didn't prove any immediate danger and the ultimate loss of the bow thruster was nothing more than losing a luxury for docking, I was deeply concerned about the stabilizers. We were currently in flat seas but not for long. At the very least, we had to deal with The Beaufort, Chukchi, and Bering Seas which would batter us with a ferocity which we hadn't yet experienced. At that time of year, seas between twenty feet and thirty feet were not unheard of.

Without stabilizers, *Bagan* would be tossed mercilessly and in high seas she would have absolutely no means of stabilizing herself from the havoc. If all continued to go as planned, we'd be in Resolute Bay inside of a few weeks and could arrange to have the new pump shipped to us there. The Arctic area we were passing through now is usually under the influence of a high pressure system, so the odds of anything sneaking up on us were considerably less than had we been farther south. But the combination of the extreme isolation we were soon to be heading into, vague and incomplete nautical charts, potentially dangerous seas with no means of stabilization, and ice were far from comforting.

Clinton broke out the schematics for the hydraulic system, found the pump number as well as the phone number for the factory and set about to place a call to them to hunt down and arrange to have the pump shipped.

If only it could be that simple.

Once again the cold granite in my stomach was back with a vengeance. The last two days of bliss were a step away from the continuing and relentless stress. If Clinton could get a connection on our satellite phone, sometimes it wouldn't last more than a few seconds. Not being able to upload pictures or blogs was one thing. Potentially losing our link to civilization was entirely another. We were not in immediate trouble, but I now realized that our "guaranteed" link to outside help had just been taken from us. That haunting feeling I had the night before was back. Now, more than ever, we truly were on our own.

CHAPTER 9

INTO THE PASSAGE: THE BACK SIDE OF THE MOON

Forty-five days after leaving Newport, on July 31, 2009, at 8:30 a.m., we crossed into the Northwest Passage.

In the blink of an eye, everything changed, yet oddly, everything felt the same.

The first third of the trip was over and because of all the incredible beauty, daily problems, and settling—or not—of all the squabbles, my fantasies had completely overlooked what I would feel.

As we headed deeper into Lancaster Sound, the countdown of the last few hundred yards, then feet, started, the cheer went up, the cake was cut into, and my eyes and mind were telling me that like Alice, we had moved through a "Looking Glass" of historic proportions. Within seconds, the stakes of the trip had tripled.

With a slice of Northwest Passage cake in hand, I went up to the boat deck to try to come to grips with what had just happened. Settling in between crates of supplies, dive gear, and various odds and ends, I looked back at *Bagan*'s wake as she was getting farther away from the familiar and into what I could only describe to myself as the back side of the moon. The door had shut behind us with no hesitation, and any sight or vestige of the safety and control we had only minutes earlier was now seemingly gone. *Bagan* was still gliding along at her eight knots, the six of us were still united in our goal to find our way through The Passage to the Beaufort Sea and beyond. But now we were on our own.

The southern cliffs of Devon Island to our north were Martian. Sharp contrasting layers and ridges rose up from water's edge hundreds of feet above us. Sheer, raw earth with very little evidence of vegetation ran mile after mile down to the west, untouched. The wind would be calm, then in a blink would be sharp, edged, ice cold, and thirty knots, then return to calm. The water was in the mid-thirties, coarse, raw, deep blue, and far from comforting.

We were ushered further into Lancaster Sound by a pod of four orcas, their six-foot dorsal fins slicing through the water, not in the usual, friendly manner that you can see in the Pacific Northwest, but with a determined impersonal agenda.

With video camera in hand, Chauncey joined me on the boat deck to grab a shot of these killer whales. "Jesus, you fall in the water here, it's over," he said.

There was no backing out now.

As Chauncey and I talked, I could see small breaths—like wispy ghosts—escaping our mouths. The temperature had dropped quickly and although the strength of the Arctic sun was evident, it did little to warm us. It had all changed so quickly, the hills, plateaus, and even the waves lapping at the shore had a more menacing feel.

I went below and sliding the hatch door shut, I tried to close out all those troubling feelings and thoughts that were swamping me.

It was no different below. As we made our way up to the south shore of Devon Island, there was nothing but reverent silence in the pilothouse. No joking, no bitching, no music, no chatter. Everyone was aware that we had entered a hallowed and potentially dangerous part of the world. It took no imagination to picture Franklin and his ships or the scores who attempted transit before and the many who came later searching for him as they sailed deeper into Lancaster Sound.

Just as it was more than 150 years earlier, there were no channel markers to warn us of hidden shoals. We did have the incredible advantage of modern day electronics, but all it takes is one glitch. We were now among ghosts. The hundreds of men who failed here were around us, watching in silence.

We decided to work our way north a bit and up along the south shore of the island. Our next intended anchorage was Blaney Bay and that was still a good thirty-six hours off.

From outside on deck, with great volume, Greg shouted, "Polar bear on shore!" Lens caps flying, tripods adjusted, gasping we inched up on our first polar bear. With the lightness of a small dog, not a thousand-pound, nine-foot predator, he would easily climb up and down the layered hills behind him, paying us absolutely no heed.

Shortly we came across two other smaller polar bears lying down, partially hidden on shore by lichen-covered boulders. Every bit the same color as the cliffs they sat in front of—perfect camouflage for the world's perfect predator.

These bears can swipe the head off a seal in a snap, swim hundreds of miles, and have even been documented hiding behind a small block of ice as they stealthily push it ahead of them, inching up on unsuspecting sleeping seals.

For the rest of that day and through the night we hugged the shoreline of Devon Island and made our way deeper into The Passage. The scenery became increasingly basic, rugged, offering up nothing we'd ever seen. Lancaster Sound occasionally hosts passages of an Inuit fishing party, but there was no evidence of that in our immediate area. We first came upon the ice around 2 a.m., spotted by Sefton, low-lying, pale blue, jagged, and bumpy sheets of ice. From our perspective of a few miles off, it appeared impenetrable. Yet, when we slowly motored up and into it, we saw that the small floes were scattered widely enough to allow easy, albeit careful and deliberate, passage through it. Silence overtook the boat as we all stared in amazement. Some sheets were no more than inches high, others rose twenty feet, hosting seals and Arctic terns. It was an easy trail through, wide enough to not have to alter course but narrow enough to command full attention. The midnight sun was casting its pale, haunting blue hue over the entire area. Brown hills, rocky and gray shores, impassive sheets of ice, and even *Bagan* was bathed in a color more death than pastel. No words needed to be exchanged to know that all of us were officially in an area where finality and luck were on equal playing fields.

The sense of adventure still fueled us, enough so that all petty arguments and conflicts seemed a part of a long-gone history. I could sense everyone rising to what was now at hand.

At 4 a.m., we motored into a deep and narrow bay which, having a moving, living glacier at its head, was the logical place to stop, drop the hook, rest, and check the ice charts. With not much to go on for depth soundings, Clinton maneuvered *Bagan* to the face of the glacier and shut her down. There we sat as we listened to the deep groans, cracks, and shifting of the massive glacier that easily reached 100 feet at its head. We watched and listened as the midnight sun slowly rose over the area, changing the pale blue, white, and brown face of this moving ice mountain to a deeper blue and whiter white. Dark, brooding shadows changed from soft blue to pink to gray as the sun all but kissed the horizon and started its path back up into the Arctic sky. Chauncey was on the foredeck and Clinton and I were in the pilothouse trying to read a bare chart; Dominique and Sefton were getting geared up and readying cameras when we heard it.

A deep roar. Clinton and I looked at each other, knowing it wasn't the glacier. "What the fuck?" In an instant, the others charged through the pilothouse out to the stern.

"Walruses."

By this time, all had become so adept with the cameras that video was with zero delay. *Bagan* was drifting nicely down toward a gathering of perhaps fifteen walruses. Amazingly, in the distance we could see an approaching, massive polar bear with blood stained muzzle and chest. Every few minutes, he'd stop, lift his head, take in a full sniff, and continue toward the unsuspecting group. Unaware, these walruses sat in the shallows, occasionally lowering their heads and massive white tusks to dig up the bottom and perhaps see what there was to feed on. We watched the bear, he watched the walruses, and the walruses watched no one in particular—a true *National Geographic* moment. I have to admit that what I thought was going to happen in mere moments wasn't something I thought I'd have the stomach for—survival in the wild, the time-honored food chain. Walruses are known for their incredibly thick hides and a kill was not going to be swift and sure, but protracted and brutal.

The bear kept his steady pace, stopping occasionally to hone in on his prey, but something different caught his keen sense of smell. He lifted his head even higher, pulling in another offering, tasting of air, and slowly turned toward *Bagan*, and all we had in the way of food, garbage, fish scents, and "boat smells" had grabbed his olfactory sensors with full and immediate attention. For a moment his focus was us, a fact wasted on no one aboard *Bagan* that morning.

Greg was next to me snapping stills. For more than ten minutes, no one said anything more than a whispered word or two. Seeing the polar bear take in an even larger sniff of us, not 100 yards away, Greg lowered his camera for just a moment and uttered, "Shit." I agreed wholeheartedly. No one moved and all watched wondering if we were simply a curiosity or actually a player in the developing scenario.

Taking a fresh sniff of the walruses, the bear started to climb the low rise behind them and once directly in back, perhaps fifty yards away, hunkered down like a cat before a pounce. The bear didn't shift weight or tense muscles for an expected leap, but sat with laser-like black, cold eyes focused on the scene in the water below him.

It was simply a matter of time.

Dominique, who was by now on the bow, saw that while our position was a perfect one for capturing the about-to-unfold drama, *Bagan* was drifting slowly onto shallow rocks. Nothing of immediate danger, but enough to know we needed to maneuver to one side or the other of the coming shallows. Clinton fired the bow thruster to move *Bagan* from the shore and the noise, thankfully, was enough to alert all concerned. The polar bear quickly headed south, the walruses north and we sat happy, away from all the rocks, with plenty of spectacular footage that held no death or struggle. After dropping the hook, eating, and grabbing some sleep, Greg, Chauncey, and Sefton took to Big Black and wound their way directly among the same pack of walruses, which had moved down shore. Even now they were every bit as oblivious to our presence. Amazingly, the three quietly powered among them getting moving shots from no more than ten feet away. It was remarkable footage and watching it later the next morning filled me even more with a sense of pride, purpose, and accomplishment. We were in the Northwest Passage and with that were getting rarely seen footage. Maybe all the problems and conflicts were left outside in Baffin Bay and we were now all wonderfully focused on the task at hand.

Later in the day, we once again headed west into The Passage to an area that for me was Ground Zero for the whole trip. Beechy Island was one of the last known stops of the doomed Franklin Expedition and it was there in what is now called Erebus Bay that his ships the *HMS Erebus* and *HMS Terror* were locked in frozen ice for two years. Shortly after their departure from here, history shows that they made it a bit farther south to the northwest area of King William Island but, save for a few scattered artifacts and relics, sawed bones, and occasional ship's timbers, nothing is known about the demise of the 128 aboard and the two state-of-the-art ships. These men were the heroes of their era, equivalent to the astronauts of our day. Charged to find a route through the unforgiving Northwest Passage, they simply disappeared.

To bring *Bagan* into this very bay where Franklin and his men waited out two frozen and desolate years was going to be the pinnacle of any experience I'd had to date. To anchor *Bagan* near where the *Erebus* and *Terror* were anchored, for me, would be an honor and privilege second to none. If all went well for the next twenty-four hours, not only would I be anchored in the lap of maritime history, I would be doing so with my children.

In Beechy Island, Clinton and I felt it best to start getting in touch with a man who had, over the past year, become my email friend—Peter Semotiuk, an electrical engineer and resident of Cambridge Bay, a small Inuit community in Nunavut, Canada, that sits about halfway through The Passage. Cambridge Bay is a traditional stopping place for research vessels that ply The Passage. For years, Peter has been the unofficial "ice guru" for The Passage.

Over single side band radio, he has advised research vessels of the ice's seasonal flow, and offered opinions on trends. At one point, Peter kept the skipper of a very small boat overwintering in the ice outside The Passage constant company, helping him to endure the mind-numbing and brutal tortures of an Arctic winter.

During the past year, I'd been in touch with Peter through email about our plans. It was time to check in with him and get his thoughts about how this summer's ice was shaping up. Peter would be able to look long range, and based on his history and personal connection with the Arctic, he would play a large part in whether we should continue with the trip or try to turn back, if we could.

On August 2 at 2 p.m., we dropped the hook in Erebus Bay on Beechy Island. The day's travel had been as the past few, less than ten knots of air and flat seas. We'd paralleled the southern coastline of Devon Island, came upon Beechy Island on the southwest tip, and slowly worked our way north to Erebus Bay. I sat glued to the helm chair in the pilothouse not knowing what to expect. As the coastline opened into the bay, I sat frozen in awe.

In front of us was the deep, rounded bay where 128 men, who set out with nothing more than orders and courage, endured two winters only to vanish before the next. Research vessels and a smattering of other specially designed vessels had come and gone since 1845, but almost all of the evidence of their presence was lost to the killer winters. Yet the invisible presence of Franklin and his men was immediate, still felt and perhaps even seen.

We lazily circled the bay looking for the best depth and holding ground. All six crew were assembled at various places about our modern and small ship, almost one-third the size of Franklin's, all silent in the press of the weight of the maritime tragedy that started to unfold in this bay.

In the north of the bay and not far from the shore were the four head-stones, grave markers which through drawings of the day or photographs brought back in the last century, marked the first of the Franklin Expedition members to die. While there always was much speculation about their deaths, it wasn't until 1981 when Owen Beattie, a professor of anthropology, exhumed the graves and performed full autopsies. The bodies were in perfect condition, frozen in the positions they were laid more than 165 years ago.

Beattie's photographs showed haunted and weathered faces and bodies that had succumbed, in his professional estimation, to pneumonia and tuberculosis hastened by lead poisoning. As we were to see in the coming days, discarded meat tins from Franklin's expedition were still scattered about the site and it was hauntingly obvious to see that these tins, at their joints, had heavy and bulky lead welds for joining the halves together, a factor that assuredly contributed to the ultimate failure of the trip.

Beattie was to later find in maritime records that Franklin and company had taken the lowest bid of meat packers who, at the time, weren't well-versed with the soldering of food tins.

We dropped hook and settled in immediately. Greg and I started to talk about a dive. There was talk and excitement of a shore party to explore and film but my wanting to get in the water and get footage of what perhaps few others, if any, had ever seen before, was first and foremost. Greg and I broke out all the gear, the underwater communication was checked and rechecked, thermals, boots, dry suits, and face masks donned. Dry suits are a royal pain in the ass. We had planned to acquire and fit my suits earlier and do some winter diving off of Newport, but Greg wasn't able to get the suit until a week before departure.

Rubberneck seals, wrist seals, and ankle seals grip tightly and start cutting off your circulation if you stand around on deck too long. Once below and in the water, weight starts to compress your body and the seals loosen just a tad, not enough to allow water in, but enough to allow blood to circulate.

I was first into the thirty-degree water. Greg always likes to hang back and make sure his diving partner is in and squared away before he gets in. I watched below as he pulled down his full-face mask, pressed the "to talk" buttons (although I heard him and he me, this was the first and last time these would work successfully) and in he came. As we were descending through the fifty-foot water column, I adjusted the camera housing, when it felt as though someone was sticking a knife down in my wrist seal, and after a search for any encroaching and unwanted sea critters, I realized that this sharp-cutting action was nothing more than a minute amount of the freezing Arctic water working its way down past the seal. All dry suits leak to one degree or another, but I hadn't expected the temperature of the water to be hovering around freezing. As these intrusive drops of water worked their way down my arm, I felt the sharp, stinging pain one would get from a block of dry ice. But another sensation, a hot searing pain that all but had me yelping, was coming from a very familiar spot, my toe. The thermal layers, drysuit material, and heavy dive fin were succumbing to the pressure of the depth and pushing in on my feet and my toe was reacting as it had during the past few months. To try to kick or use my fin was beyond painful, debilitating, and discouraging, but I simply couldn't acknowledge it now. I was fifty feet down in Erebus Bay, a place I'd held in my dreams since I was a child and the discomfort was paled by comparison to the thrill of the accomplishment.

Greg and I swam in general widening and lazy circles, not looking for anything in particular and just trying to get an overall sense of the geography and makeup of the bottom. Apart from a scattering of marine life, a few small clams, sea urchins, small snakes, and worms, it was featureless. Unfortunately, I began to think about some advice we'd received before we left Halifax from a wonderful guy named Todd Burlingame, a man who'd spent the majority of his life in the Arctic. "Remember the polar bears," he said, "they can swim ... far and very fast."

With that sobering thought in mind, we went further into the bay, always, for me at least, turning around every few minutes.

More water trickled past my wrist seal, causing a small gasp of breath as it froze its way down. I realized what would happen were one of our regulators to blow or rupture; although we were only at fifty feet, an easy and controlled assent, I had no idea what the freezing water would have done to the back of our throats.

That thought shifted quickly, for now I'd passed into something totally unexpected and far more powerful than freezing water at the back of my throat. If ever there were a place where one could swim among ghosts, this was it. I felt I was being watched, I felt the presence of time and tragedy wafting through the water. I'm not usually drawn to things that go bump in the night, but I do give full credence to the possibility of wandering souls and spirits.

There was a tangible feeling that we were not alone. I looked up from time to time, knowing I would see nothing though I would not have been surprised if I had.

We surfaced and never was I more glad to see four smiling, alive, and familiar faces. The sight of Clinton with rifle in hand gave me great relief that while we were away, our backs were always covered. Climbing out of all the gear and finally on deck standing in the waning Arctic light, I knew that my life had changed forever. To this day, I can't tell you exactly why or how, but after the fifty minutes under the water at Beechy Island, I came out far from the person I was when I'd entered.

I'd been allowed to be a part of a rich and tragic maritime history and will never forget the grace and acceptance I felt as I was permitted to enter.

For the rest of my life, I will know that I was a part of something unexplained, spiritual, and remarkably powerful during that dive.

Once out of my suit, I was relieved to see that the cutting sensation that I'd had at the beginning of the dive in my wrist area was indeed prompted by a small amount of water that had worked itself in. I wasn't as relieved when I finally got a chance to see my toe. It looked healthy and pink, but the pain was searing. By this time in the trip, I knew I had a problem that I felt best not to share with anyone. The trip had been hard and was going to get harder. I couldn't afford any of the crew to question my mental or physical health.

At 11 p.m. that night, bathed in eerie blue-gray shadows, Chauncey, Sefton, Greg, and Clinton went ashore to grab some shots and explore. By this point, we always had two crew members with guns whose job it was to look for polar bears.

What was supposed to be a few hours of filming turned into an eight-hour stay. The light was ethereal, the pressing weight of history and tragedy everywhere. The graves silently waited. When they finally returned, they all said how powerful and otherworldly the time ashore was. They said that, like me in the water below, they never felt alone, and felt they were being watched.

In a video I watched after the trip, Sefton talks to the camera. In the background you could see the Franklin graves. Sefton's face was drawn, wane, ghostly pale, bathed by the bluish cast from the altering of the Arctic midnight sun. As the footage rolls, Sefton gathers his thoughts, tries to talk and stops. He tries again, looking everywhere but into the lenses and says softly, "We're on Beechy Island, Erebus Bay." He pauses to look around nervously, then continues, haltingly, "This is hands-down the scariest, spookiest place I've ever been. We're on the back side of the moon, Mars."

After their shoot, they all climbed into Big Black, silent in what they'd just been a part of. As they approached the boat, Sefton turned around and saw, perhaps fifty feet away, a polar bear sniffing at where the tripod had been. The bear had been watching, cleverly hidden, not yards away the entire time they were ashore. And with not a boulder or ridge in this flat expanse to hide behind, the two gun carriers had missed him. Everyone aboard Big Black froze with the thought of what could have been.

As the bear pawed and sniffed the ground, Sefton said, "Okay, now it's personal!"

Soon after arriving back on *Bagan*, Greg saw hundreds of pale, white ghosts, silently making their way into the wide and empty bay. No sound, no disturbance in the water, but body after body slowly and very deliberately silently rolling through the bay's opening and into shore; easily more than

500 belugas were intent on their passage and completely oblivious to our presence.

Everyone climbed back aboard Big Black and with cameras and dive gear at hand, proceeded to get into the pack and silently travel among them. The belugas were into the shallows to rub up against the rough bottom and scrape dead skin and parasites off their gleaming white bodies with stealthy and natural grace. The next day they returned and did it again, present-day ghosts among ghosts from a different era, ghosts from a brutal and tragic time, a history to which *Bagan* and crew were now inexorably linked.

CHAPTER 10

THE GHOSTS OF BEECHY ISLAND

The email from our ice guru, Peter Semotiuk, was short and to the point. "The ice is late in opening this year, no trend showing. Don't go too far south, but be ready."

This news brought us some needed extra time since it was still a few days before our hydraulic pump was to arrive in Resolute Bay. Our time on Beechy Island had been a gift. The flip side of that remarkable experience was that we knew that all indications suggested it was time to leave now.

Consulting the charts, Clinton suggested we keep going north and head to what appeared to be an open and inviting anchorage called Griffin Inlet. This anchorage would place us just over the 75th parallel, 900 miles south of the North Pole. With nothing more in mind than an interesting entry in our log book and extremely rare experience, we left Beechy Island paying our own, silent, and deep respect to those we were leaving behind in Erebus Bay and headed north for Griffin Inlet.

It was no more than a good day's run, but we soon discovered that as far north as we were, with every mile we advanced, the terrain and scenery became increasingly more bleak, barren, and incapable of supporting most life.

Two days earlier, I would have said it impossible for our surroundings to get any more hostile and formidable. But working our way north up Wellington Channel, we became increasingly smaller and less significant. A fifty-seven–foot fiberglass boat with six lives aboard was trivial compared to the raw power around us. Rugged, empty hills appeared to have just been formed, seemingly still moving and settling.

We were in a frozen vacuum. An uncharted shoal could easily throw all sixty tons of our ship up on her ear and there we would sit, indefinitely. A blown engine or bent shaft and the game is over.

We'd all agreed before we left Newport that if we got into serious trouble, we'd try to escape it without seeking the aid of the Coast Guard or research vessels. No one told us to venture to The Passage and we were not going to seek help from others. In a medical emergency, I wouldn't hesitate in trying to call Phil Wagner, our land-based doctor who had given Dominique her emergency medical training. But shy of a severed limb or heart attack, the onboard feeling was, "we got ourselves into this, we will get ourselves out."

As we headed farther up Wellington Channel, the silence and awe that we all succumbed to when we arrived at Beechy Island was increased tenfold. The air temperature had not risen above mid-thirties all day and the water temperatures hovered either side of thirty, occasionally dipping into the high-twenties. Where only hours before we saw tall, sharp, and jagged cliffs with little color, we now cruised alongside a more flattened terrain devoid of any hue. Aboard *Bagan*, everything seemed black and white. Onboard enthusiasm was slowly turning to heavy concern and what yesterday were eyes of wonder and smiles of astonishment were now lines of studied concentration and heightened senses.

As we rounded into the anchorage at Griffin Inlet, I felt I had no right to be in that anchorage, that I was unqualified for such an honor. There was a small element of fatality in the air—a feeling that the thin line between live or die was frighteningly obvious.

The author.

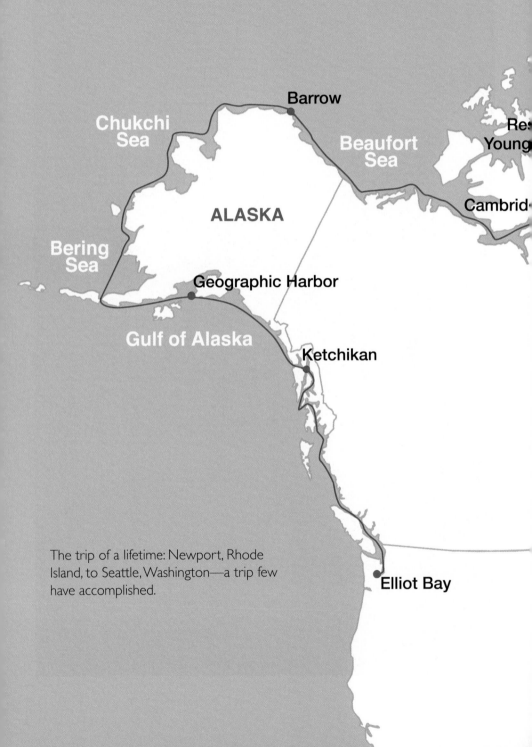

Barrow

Chukchi
Sea

Beaufort
Sea

Re:
Young

ALASKA

Cambrid

Bering
Sea

Geographic Harbor

Gulf of Alaska

Ketchikan

The trip of a lifetime: Newport, Rhode
Island, to Seattle, Washington—a trip few
have accomplished.

Elliot Bay

Vigilance for marauding polar bears was vital when we were trapped in the ice.

My stepchildren, Dominique and Chauncey Tanton, on ice watch as we made our way up Greenland's west coast.

Disko Bay, Greenland. *Bagan* explores some of the mountainous castoff bergs from Greenland's massive inland ice sheet.

"Big Black," our twenty-foot inflatable, inspects one of the most unusual bergs we encountered. Note the "face" on the right side, watching in mute testimony.

With underwater camera housing in hand, Greg DeAscentis surfaces after inspecting for hull damage after our first harrowing day battling the ice.

Once trapped, we anchored on the ice and moved with it to prevent it from sliding by and ripping *Bagan's* hull.

Before leaving Disko Bay for the Northwest Passage, we worked our way through the area's majestic and daunting icefields.

Once through what we thought was the most treacherous part of the trip, we headed east through the Gulf of Alaska and encountered some of the worst weather I'd seen in 40,000 offshore miles.

My son, Sefton Theobald, who joined us in Halifax.

Beechy Island. The remains of Northumberland House, built as a shelter for the doomed Franklin Expedition. They never made it.

Blaney Bay. A totally disinterested herd of walrus.

The author and Clinton Bolton in the pilothouse, leaving Newport, June 16, 2009.

From left, Sefton Theobald, Chauncey Tanton, the author, and Dominique Tanton: a family reunited.

Sefton Theobald stands polar bear watch as the author and Chauncey Tanton film at Barrow, Alaska, the northernmost point of the continental United States.

You're never truly alone.

Trapped. The author looking for an exit from the ice.

Two whales in Alaska "bubble net feeding"—one of nature's more remarkable sights, and one I never thought I would witness.

Sefton Theobald trying to come to grips with the abject isolation, desolation, and brutal demands of the trip.

Hallowed grounds on Beechy Island. Graves from the doomed Franklin Expedition of 1845.

Working our way down Peel Sound as we slipped farther from all that we knew.

Nome, Alaska.
A small group
of muskox.

Greg DeAscentis: world-class photograper, diver, and friend, on Beechy Island.

Winter approaches as an arctic cold front rolls over us in the Aleutians.

Barrow, Alaska. Beauty among the death of past whale harvests.

Off in the distance, we saw a polar bear lumbering up the side of one of the rounded, rock-strewn hills. One moment he was there, the next gone. He simply disappeared into the Arctic before our eyes.

Here, in this dark and dangerous environment, the stark reality of the rest of the trip was made abundantly clear. It was a healthy feeling but it was now added to my concerns for my children, the advisability of the trip, my growing and debilitating toe problem, the water maker issue, the hydraulic pump's failure, and the intermittent satellite/internet problems.

All individual problems could be handled easily, but as a whole, they presented a growing weight, a weight I tried to not excessively share.

Having never been in this sort of leadership position before, I made the decision that while I could refer to these pressures time and again, it would be ill advised to share the deep and persistent concern they placed on me.

After setting the anchor securely in Griffin Inlet in a flat and sandy bottom, Clinton, Chauncey, Greg, and Sefton all expressed a need to get ashore, explore, and perhaps film. Reviewing safety procedures and bear-watch rules again, they set out in Big Black and headed to the distant and south side of the vast, open anchorage. The weather charts had again shown big fat isobars and what breeze we were to get would be light and variable. No sooner had Big Black gotten about 100 yards away when we were hit by thirty-five–knot winds. Knife-edged and unwavering, they howled out of the north causing *Bagan* to sail violently on the anchor. Letting out another seventy-five feet of anchor chain settled her in and, if worse came to worse, Dominique and I could always reposition *Bagan* closer to shore, more in the lee. But I was concerned for Big Black.

Even with binoculars, I had lost sight of the small shore party and after failing to see even the slightest of black dots on shore, I tried to raise them on the VHF. To my great relief they answered, and assured me all was well. They set off on their hike in the low, frozen hills while onboard Dominique started in on her never-ending job of rotating the food in the aft freezer.

We'd been gone from Newport just over a month and a half and through her method of rotation, pre-cooked stews, and ability to provide continuous variations with chicken, steak, tuna, pasta, rice, and ground beef, she had yet to repeat a dinner. As a young girl of six, Dominique would set up a "store" in one of the closets in our home. Her marketing skills being somewhat limited, her mother and I tried to encourage her sales efforts. I can remember watching hour after hour with her getting no customers let alone making any sales. Finally I asked of the family, "Would someone please buy something from that child? She has no retirement plan." I reminded her of this as she continued to shuffle our food stocks about. In the middle of moving her previously cooked meals to the back and meat to the front she paused, grinned, and again said, "Oh my God, you remember that?" Above the Arctic Circle and seemingly hundreds of miles from any form of human life, we shared a soft, loving laugh and distant memory, that six-year-old girl and I.

With a large mug of black tea in hand, I settled into the helm seat in the pilothouse, hunkered down from the constant and howling winds outside, and started back in on some magazine articles I was writing about the trip. My mind elsewhere and finding an excuse not to write, I grabbed binoculars to try to keep an eye on the shore party. Dominique had just finished her repacking of the freezer and was about to head down for a nap. The wind hadn't abated but *Bagan* was a bit more under control, not swinging so wildly. On her way past me, Dominique stopped, looked straight ahead out the pilothouse windows, and said without turning to me, "Sprague, this is a bad place. We shouldn't be here." We both stood thinking and knowing that we both understood what she'd just said. Were the words coming from my six-year-old stepdaughter that'd be one thing, I'd know what to do; picking her up, putting her in my lap, and making some sort of reassuring talk usually solved fears and concerns. But the fact that these feelings were coming from a grown and sea-wise woman was entirely another matter.

The best I could offer up was, "I know, kiddo, we won't be here for long." I gave her a hug and went up to the bridge deck to think about what she'd just said. She was right. From the moment we left Beechy, I knew we were heading into a place where we weren't wanted, and now that we'd settled in and were on the hook, that feeling grew by the minute.

I stood, looked about the hills, and watched as the wind tore up the Arctic water around us. I wondered how any man survived such raw and powerful elements. Physical survival was one thing; the ability to mentally endure amazed me. I rubbed my eyes, thinking I had a "floater" in my eye— as a small gray blob was moving about in my field of vision. It seemed to be the only thing moving for miles. I rubbed my eyes again, looked again, and now saw that this speck was on land and had most assuredly moved, or maybe it hadn't. Looking through the binoculars, I could see not much better nor get a more precise definition of what the blob was and if it actually did move or not.

I quickly panned the glasses to the south and perhaps a mile away could see the shore party on the ridge of one of the hills that ran down to the anchorage. Sweeping the glasses back up and to the north, I again saw the white form but, as before, I could not tell if it had moved or not. It was that far away. Perhaps it was just a large boulder?

Calling the shore party on the VHF on the flying bridge brought no answer. I called again, "*Bagan* to shore party, *Bagan* to shore party ... *Bagan* to shore party ... over." No answer. I went below to the pilothouse and tried to raise them again but with the same result. Over the course of thirty minutes I tried this several more times, each time in vain. Looking again through the glasses at the white form, I wasn't sure if it had moved again.

Ninety minutes later I saw Big Black pounding through the wind-driven seas and heading home. By now, the northwest breeze was occasionally peaking at forty knots and while *Bagan* was secure as always, Big Black was earning her money, as were the four waterlogged crew aboard.

Once they were all settled aboard and dried out, I had to ask if they'd heard me about my overly concerned "bear" sighting. I felt like the angry parent whose child has come home late. I was trying not to let my voice register anger or frustration. As I remember, Clinton's answer was as infuriating as it was arrogant, "Yeah, I heard you but who had the better view for a bear, you or me on the ridge and with a gun. Gimme a break." I strongly suggested to him that even a bogus warning was better than none and asked if he'd preferred that in the future I simply ignore all bear sightings, real or not? He walked down to his cabin without another word. I turned to look at the others, "Guys, in the future, when someone calls on the VHF, it should always be acknowledged, regardless of who has the radio." Their silence told me that they agreed.

At noon the next day and after once again consulting weather and ice charts, we decided to up-anchor and make our way down to Resolute Bay with hopes of picking up the much-needed hydraulic pump. Our time in Griffin Inlet had not been a comfortable one and all agreed that perhaps this was about as far north as we wanted to head. Any farther north and we would be tempting fate, sticking our collective thumbs in the eye of caution.

We did notice on the latest weather chart that the wind was going to trend out of the east for the next few days which raised some concern. A shift in direction held the potential for any ice blown east and past Resolute to be blown back in. For now it was light and variable and out of the north but it was a shift that held far more promise of trouble than it normally would in Narragansett Bay off Newport.

We hadn't been underway for more than a few hours when I heard the unmistakable sound of our engine being throttled back. This rarely means good things, so I ventured up to the pilothouse hoping to see a pod of whales, pack of dolphins, gaggle of geese, anything but what I saw.

During the past thirty minutes, we had worked our way down onto and were now paralleling a scattered but thick field of ragged and dark, pale blue ice. While this wasn't our first encounter, it had a feel to it like none other. It appeared old, torn up, and permanent. The further we paralleled it, the thicker it became and we'd now come to that point where we were picking our way through it. By no means was it a trip-stopper, but as all of our faces showed, this was the real thing and not just another photo-op. I took the helm from Clinton while he tried to get online and download the latest offering from the Canadian Ice Service. What we saw as it filled one of the pilothouse computer monitors was sobering and deeply concerning.

Since the last reading of the ice chart, what was a distant and scattered field of ice far off to the west in Barrow Straight had worked its way past and into Resolute Bay, shutting off all possibility of entering or leaving.

On closer examination, we could see that the bay itself had more than 50 percent coverage and we could only imagine what was becoming of the boats that were already in there. There was now no point trying to work our way into Resolute. The guarantee of getting out in one piece was minimal at best. After a protracted discussion, we decided to try to move south into Peel Sound far earlier than planned and find a safe and secure anchorage.

It was about this time that Chauncey asked about the gas situation for Big Black. Up until then I hadn't been told that there was a "situation" so I listened as he claimed that we had perhaps a gallon of fuel left for her. I looked at Clinton; he was silent on the matter. Coldly I asked if this were true and if so how long had people known?

Unfortunately, the answers I got were far from what I wanted to hear. Yes, we only had about a gallon, maybe a gallon and a half, left. That should be "enough." Enough for us to do what? I thought back onto the night ashore in Sisimiut and all the side trips of exploration and fun. Did those running the boat not take into consideration the fuel needs? One and a half gallons was far from the comfort level I wanted. Chauncey immediately volunteered to take Big Black through the ice into Resolute and get more fuel. Chauncey is and always has been a man of his own mind. So many times as a kid I'd see him bump up against a self-imposed wall and barrel straight ahead trying to breach the problem his way. When it works, it is a wonderful personality trait, when it doesn't, it goes against you and creates a possibility of alienating those around you. This was what we were now beginning to experience.

Clinton and I tried to point out that if he made it, there would be no guarantee that he would make it out, with the very real possibility of needing more fuel trying to find his way in through the thick ice pack. Ultimately, he acquiesced but not before quietly blaming Clinton's poor management, something that did not sit well with Clinton.

I didn't know it at the time, but this mild but determined assignment of blame was to spark a problem between the two that would come to a head down the road when we least needed it.

We decided to suck it up, move farther south into Peel Sound and anchor for a few days hoping for an opening in the "central ice," the Passage-choking ice to the south.

The trend we thought we'd seen a few days earlier had reversed itself and at that moment there was no getting anywhere near where we needed to go in order to reach Cambridge Bay, our next planned stop where we needed to take on diesel for *Bagan's* needs.

At 8:30 that evening, we abandoned hopes of getting into Resolute Bay to retrieve the spare pump and entered Peel Sound, getting even deeper and more committed to transiting The Passage. We were now moving into the body of water where ships and souls who failed in their attempts to transit The Passage either turned around or abandoned ship and took to the land.

The names of the coves and passages read like a memorial service for failed attempts: Bellot Straight, Fury Beach, Boothia Peninsula, McClintock Sound.

The trip had become one of deadly earnest as we entered Peel Sound. The odds of success had become massively stacked against us. It was simple: if the ice to the south didn't open, we weren't going to make it through, if Resolute Bay didn't clear, we couldn't get needed diesel or gas for the engines. And if we did have to turn back and limp into Greenland, we had the soon-to-be-forming autumn Atlantic gales to contend with. Perversely on time, the failing hydraulic pump in the engine room once again blew past its bearings and made a screeching, rattling noise, which reminded us all we were on borrowed time.

Here I got my first taste of dwindling options. If we couldn't get into Resolute, we weren't going to be able to pick up the new pump. Clinton decided that once we got settled into our next anchorage, he'd start myriad satellite phone cells to see what our options would be.

Our new aim was to head for Howe Harbor on the east side of Peel Sound. It was protected, seemingly ice-free, and wide enough to allow for an easy, relatively speaking, exit if the ice was to start heading south down the sound. It was perhaps twenty-four hours away and judging by the ice charts, there was none between it and us. But to get far enough south to this protected stopover, we needed to navigate and work our way through the small offerings of pack ice in Peel Sound that were moving up from the south. It was still spread out enough to allow us room to maneuver and always presented many workable paths, though it was to give us our first and most sobering experience of the deadly potential that it held.

No longer were we gliding through the thin sheet ice that we'd experienced earlier that day, always keeping far enough away from any concentration so as not to present a problem. Now we were dealing with ice that was solid, old, hard as cement and offered hidden ten-foot shelves under the water, shelves that you didn't see until you were upon them.

So far it'd all been manageable—maneuvering wide-open leads into and out of this scattering of ice was predictable and easily seen in the distance. The tension had been raised earlier over the gas situation but now, although lessened a bit, had simply transferred to our getting through the fat and open maze. We were all beginning to relax, and become accustomed to the Arctic's latest offering when both Greg and Dominique let out howls of amazement. Just off our starboard bow, not 100 yards away, atop a floe perhaps 300 feet long and equally as wide, was a fully twelve-foot grown polar bear. He had seen us way before Greg and Dominique saw him and was now drinking in the smells that I'm sure were pouring from *Bagan*. He must have remained standing for thirty seconds or more and with perfect timing dropped only to all fours as soon as cameras were rolling.

Our presence did nothing to disturb this amazing creature. He was clearly attentive to us, pacing the ice, perhaps trying to time his best opportunity to leap or swim to the source of all the great smells. Clinton maneuvered *Bagan* to within 100 feet, all the while keeping an eye on the depth gauges and overview of the ice pack on the radar.

My concern, apart from a 900-pound bear that was showing a great interest in us, was the ice off our stern. As we'd seen before, all it would take would be a subtle but steady shift of wind and we could quickly be locked in with the object of our photographic intentions. He had brought out his whole repertoire of tricks and poses: on all fours, butt in the air like a puppy, sitting Buddha-like, hunkered down with paws over black nose. He showed us every pose in the book. I was sure he was trying to lure us closer.

Watching and filming this guy was a wonderful distraction for the building problems at hand. These problems fed the by-now familiar tensions, which as the days were to unfold would take me into a far deeper and darker place than I would have ever wanted to go.

CHAPTER 11

STUCK

I was stunned.

Peter's email had literally knocked the wind out of me. It felt as though I was watching a 1950s B-movie with terrible special effects, but as I read and reread Peter's sobering words, my ears were filled with the rush and roar of time.

"Danger of Peel Sound getting capped over with ice to the north, keep an eye on it. Bellot Straight is iced in." In that short handful of words, he let me know that if the central ice in The Passage south of us did not open in time for us to get through, and with one escape route now blocked and the other perhaps soon to be blocked, we were sitting on the edge of a very bad situation—failure or worse. The familiar, cold granite feeling in my stomach was back with a vengeance.

The duality of my role, trip leader as well as parent, was starting to split and head in two distinctly separate and inexorably diverging paths. If I had a crew of seasoned pros, it would be easy. I could simply announce we were facing a predicament that held serious repercussions. But these were my children, and I didn't want to raise any more alarm than necessary. I needed to protect my children.

I've always been a great believer in having Plans B, C, and D. If the original plan goes awry, which it usually does, I've always taken great comfort in following the alphabet all the way down to Z if necessary. Reading Peter's email, I realized that my Plans B and C had just been snatched off the table, seemingly before they ever got there.

Somewhere in the back of my mind lurked a Plan D.

For a few days, we had been slowly moving south into Peel Sound, crisscrossing the twenty miles of its width, moving from one anchorage to another, all the while waiting to see some indication of a lead opening up in the ice charts. Peter's emails continued to be straight and to the point: the seasonal opening was running late and if it were going to happen this year, it may be brief. We were now facing the point of no return. The crew and I had all had conversations about the potential of not being able to get through and at one point Clinton and I actually projected dates when we'd need to turn around. If we weren't to reach Cambridge Bay by September 2, there would be no point at all in trying to punch on through to Barrow then. By then, the Bering Sea would be in full voice and even the 100-foot commercial fishing vessels would have their hands full.

That date we all agreed on. What Clinton and I discussed privately was the scenario of Peel Sound being iced over to the north, trapping us for at least the winter. Neither of us had any answers for such a scenario and tried to keep focused on what we knew, not what we were guessing. Over the next ten days, we moved from small anchorage to small anchorage. Howe Harbor, Hummock Point, Pandora Island, and Young Bay. Featureless, foggy, and indifferent. We were playing for time as the clock was ticking. Every day we spent on "this" side of the central ice meant we had one less for "that" side. If we were late into getting through, the odds for the success decreased as dramatically as the power of the gales from autumn storms might increase. We read, we slept, we watched DVDs, and we coaxed every number out of the ice charts we could.

By moving in twenty-mile hops down through Peel Sound, we were trying to position ourselves as close to the central channel ice pack as we could, hoping to take immediate advantage of even the slightest of leads. But by getting that close, we were allowing ourselves dangerous exposure. If the wind shifted suddenly south, the ice would be blown up onto us. This we judged by looking at wind charts two or three times per day as we tried to predict systems forming as far away as Siberia.

We'd watch their development and see if we needed to act accordingly by retreating north. Tensions were mounting and while all aboard did a remarkable job of keeping a lid on things, it was a potentially volatile atmosphere that could change over the most innocuous of comments. I fell back on the "five-minute rule." Wait five minutes before you ask a question or answer it and think about how or what you say might be misinterpreted. For the most part, the atmosphere aboard was respectful but silent yet I knew that a few of the crew were looking for a good excuse.

In Pandora Island, we were all put to one of our larger tests. We had anchored well back from the opening to Peel Sound, hopefully out of harm's way from the ice and in the lee of southeast winds. After a full dinner of cheese enchiladas, we all fell into our bunks rotating out only for anchor watch. The anchorage was as clear and empty as the land around us—flat and barren. Around five in the morning, I was awakened from a very fitful sleep to what sounded as though we were running aground. I bolted up to the pilothouse to see Sefton, who'd been on watch, out on the bow with a boat hook, pushing some small ice sheets out of the way as they slowly sailed down onto us. The wind had shifted and all the ice that was held miles up to the north in this small bay was now soon to be on top of us.

Within moments, we had up-anchored and were slowly moving over the northeast shore and inside a small arm that stuck out to the south. With not much help from the all but blank nautical charts, we felt our way into an open and secure anchorage, not 100 yards off the shore and with plenty of good mud on the bottom for holding. Once again, we settled in and started yet another day of waiting. To break the cabin-fever mood, Sefton, Chauncey, Greg, and Clinton took to the low hills to explore; Dominique and I stayed aboard to catch up and work, then later took our own small hike along the rocky shore.

By this time, my toe issues were decisively here to stay and while I'm not sure the rest of the crew ever bought my excuses, I was starting to opt out of longer hikes, explorations, and diving. To walk more than half a mile was to bring on deep cutting and searing pain.

My not being able to get off the boat and deep into the land of the Arctic was remarkably discouraging but something I had to come to terms with. I wasn't going to hike, simple as that. Dominique and I prowled along the shoreline, looking at the tiniest of living matter: weeds, crushed shells, bleached bones, and the occasional piece of small bleached-white timber. We mostly walked in silence but when the mood struck would occasionally offer something up. At one point I asked her if, in her wildest imagination, she thought that she'd ever be here, above the Arctic with her brothers. Her answer was an obvious one that was based in a large smile and a slow shake of the head. I also asked how she and Clinton were managing, how it was with Greg and her brothers. She took the Clinton question in stride and diplomatically answered, "It could be better, but we're managing." She went on to say how great it was to have Greg aboard and how he'd quickly fit in with everyone. I asked about Chauncey and Sefton. She thought a moment, looked at the boat out in the bay, up at the hills, and then continued walking. "This trip is amazing, indescribable. There's a closeness between them and me that I never expected. The trip's showing me something I didn't know we had."

We continued to walk along the shore in and out of the small wavelets, which gently lapped at the rugged and coarse red sand. I was beaming inside, because I had been feeling a connection with all three that I never knew could have existed. We had so much time to catch up on, but it felt as though we'd never been apart. In our many years of separation, I tried to keep in touch on a regular basis, calling them weekly and going to see them as often as I could. Because of their age differences, Chauncey and Dominique were occasionally out and about when I called Sefton at home. But for the most part, connections were almost always made. I tried to assure that at the end of every phone call or visit that there was a very clear understanding of the love I held for each and how much I missed them.

I thought back to my childhood, living in the same city as my father and his constant absence. As I remember it, I was always the one who had to place the call and never once did it end with an exchange of love. I'd be very hard pressed to remember a time when either my father or mother ever told me they loved me.

Often in my adult years, I thought back about how very easy it could have been for them to indulge me, tell me they loved me and perhaps even that they held a small amount of pride for me. What sort of people were they that couldn't offer this up? Why was the most basic of parental instincts so alien to them both? If they had put as much energy into expressing a love or approval of me, or my two sisters, as they did into denigrating one another in their divorced lives, what sort of adults would we three children have grown up to be? Where normal childhood memories consisted of midnight bed checks and being protected from the creatures which lurked under it, my memories were filled with middle-of-the-night drunken ramblings, a systematic, alcohol-fueled destruction of my bedroom, and extreme violation of personal boundaries, not to ever be discussed nor hinted at with either my father in the few weekends I saw him or in my mother's sober hours. How could two grown people screw up and make so very complicated the simplest of things?

Dominique's words of wonder and amazement over the growing connections with her brothers overrode the pressures and concerns of what we all were now attempting to do, the weight of this trip dissipated and the walk which she and I shared could have easily been along a well-traveled New England beach with a generational homestead waiting for us at the end.

Reality came roaring back as we walked past evidence of a makeshift grave. Someone or something had been buried not twenty feet inland, and the gravesite was marked by nothing more than a simple rock perimeter. Seeing this I felt woefully ill-prepared; we had a rifle with us but no one on dedicated bear watch. I'd badly broken one of the ship's rules. It didn't take any imagination to conjure up a possible means of death for whomever it was who lay buried under that grave. I suggested to Dominique that we should get back to the boat; she wholeheartedly agreed. During the walk, we both had the feeling that we were being watched but didn't want to say anything.

Earlier the next morning, not six hours later, Dominique and I took the same walk and came across some very fresh polar bear paw prints. Judging by the prints, the bear had walked where we had walked not hours earlier.

Shore party back aboard, another dinner in our stomachs, weather charts downloaded and studied, we fell into our routine of bed and anchor watch. Again that morning, I was awakened by the sound of what I now knew to be ice running the length of *Bagan*'s hull. I flew out of my bunk, and went out on deck. The shock of the cold, Arctic air reminded me immediately that I was still in t-shirt and boxers, not prepared for even the slightest of breezes. I could see my breath vaporizing as these small exhales escaped my mouth. But at that moment it didn't matter if I was in heavy Arctic gear or butt-naked. I saw once again we were surrounded by small sheets of ice. Nothing trip-ending, but it surrounded us and my guess was the bigger stuff was not long in coming.

We needed to get out of that anchorage and in a hurry. I quickly went back into the pilothouse and saw a sight that clearly described the levels we'd all gotten to but were afraid to talk about. It had been Dominique's watch and she was now fast asleep on one of the settees in the salon. I've done thousands of offshore miles with Dominique, everything from a Panama Canal transit to cruising in British Columbia. She's one of the best and you'd be hard-pressed to find someone to equal her dedication or enthusiasm. Seeing her asleep as she was raised no small level of anger in me but I also knew that it wasn't a case of her not being responsible. She was exhausted. Not only did she stand watches, she arranged and cooked all of our lunches and dinners. I didn't want to be the one to wake her, angry as I was. I realized we'd all been pushed to some deep limits, whether we wanted to talk about them or not. Sleep deprivation and tedium were real considerations.

Bagan was quickly underway, the morning's situation openly discussed, and once again we were heading back to the other side of the bay.

Dominique was extremely contrite about her sleeping on watch, owned up to her full responsibility, and told me clearly that she was beat. Clinton and I immediately talked of how we could adjust watch schedules to find her more time to rest between meals and try to gain strength back. She and I swapped watch schedules, and the rest modified theirs by an hour or so. While she would still stand watch, hers were limited, and rightly so. Dominique's role aboard as organizer and cook was a key, if not the most key one and she needed as much rest and energy as we could find to give her.

On August 13, we saw on the ice charts what we'd been hoping to see for days—the slightest suggestion of an opening in the ice was forming along the east shore of Peel Sound. While this wasn't anything we could act on immediately, we knew that it held more potential than anything we'd seen to date. Wanting to take advantage of this potential opening, we up-anchored and made our way farther south into Pasley Bay on the west side of the Boothia Peninsula, about three quarters of the way down Peel Sound. The opening lead was showing a definitive trend and we wanted to stage as close to it as possible in the case that it opened up wide enough for us to scoot through. If we'd learned anything about the ice, it was that it was dynamic and what it did today doesn't mean that it will do the same thing tomorrow.

Pasley Bay runs perhaps twenty miles deep into the interior of Boothia Peninsula. Steep-sided and very narrow, it offered a straight shot back into tall, empty, and desolate hills. At the mouth of the bay, we found that the bottom depth was about 100 feet and with disconcerting regularity it carried that 100 feet at least 10 miles back. By this time, we had worked our way far enough south that we were starting again to get an actual night, albeit for not more than an hour. But no longer did we have the advantage of twenty-four–hour daylight. It was close to sundown and we needed to find shallow enough anchorage that *Bagan*'s 175-pound anchor could get a good set. After several aborted attempts to set the hook, we moved even deeper into the slot of an anchorage, found water just shy of seventy-five–feet deep, and finally secured *Bagan* to the bottom for what might turn out to be a few more days of waiting. Engine off and settled, we now found that silence had once again redefined itself. There was no air or small waves. No noise to be heard and that which we ourselves created somehow was sucked into a vacuum more like that of a sound chamber than deserted anchorage.

Dominique started dinner. Clinton made log entries and the others tended to the cameras. Hoping for a chance to clear my mind of what we'd just been through and focus on what it was we were hoping to do in the next few days, I strolled out onto the deck. The cold, still Arctic night again reminded me how remarkably insignificant our presence was, that all it would take would be a landslide from the steep, loosely packed cliffs that ran the length of the bay and we'd be snuffed out in the blink of an eye.

The more I looked at the towering cliff faces around us, not fifty yards away to either side, the more I could easily envision how the slightest of tremors could seemingly fill this bay with us at the bottom. I pulled my collar up tighter against the damp night air and headed back inside to find Sefton setting the table for another one of Dominique's crock-pot wonders. The warmth and aroma of home cooking surrounded me and did wonders to lay my deadly visions to rest, for that night anyway.

Rotating through our anchor watch, we all slept the night away, hoping that the next morning's ice charts would give us a hint as to what the next move would be. That morning's report showed that while the lead hadn't reversed itself, it hadn't opened any further either, something we all willingly accepted as a day of rest that was precious to us by now. Physically we were tired, and I felt we were beginning to tap into mental reserves that weren't about to get refreshed any time soon.

Raw, searing nerve pain in my toe had awakened me that morning and kicked off a mood lower than any I'd been in to date. The anxiety from the previous day's ice struggles plus the disappointment in not being able to get into Resolute to get the needed hydraulic pump had taken a large toll and I was feeling its effect. Pissed off at the world and wanting to be anywhere but on *Bagan* semi-stuck in the Northwest Passage, I found I was now the one with attitude and needed to be off that boat quickly. I had gone to sleep feeling the pressures and fears from the day before and in the space of a few short hours, awoke with feelings of a tremendous futility and looming darkness. I wanted so badly not to be the leader in this trip any longer and would have loved to have someone to whom I could give all my concerns and feelings.

Although this inner turmoil and darkness was several stops up from where things were to eventually take me, I knew I needed to try to reframe my thinking and quickly try to make contact with some level of rational feelings. Chauncey was half asleep, half reading on the starboard settee. I walked down from the pilothouse and said, "Grab a gun, we're going ashore," and with that proceeded to Big Black to wait for him to gather his wits, Arctic gear, gun, and enthusiasm to join me. As I settled into the inflatable, I saw that during the night, the battery charger had been left out in the rain and was now sitting in a small puddle of water. At least it was fresh water, not salt. But no one had told me of the battery problem in the first place, which I found troubling. Once on shore, Chauncey and I started to walk, no direction or plan in mind. I shared my frustrations with him, "I'm sick of the trip, of the ice, the cold, the attitudes (mine included), the improvisations. I'm broke. I want to go home and knowing there's not a goddamn thing I can do about it is pissing me off to no end. The reason I don't carry a gun is that at this point I'd use it on myself."

Letting me spew my guts, Chauncey listened with great compassion and, after the air settled, simply offered back, "I know what you mean. I understand."

Sweeter words have never been spoken and I found in this grown man, this larger version of someone I used to have to discipline at the dinner table, a person of great connection and support. He offered up no specific words of encouragement nor did he need to. I knew that for all we'd been through in the past fifteen years, or more to the point, hadn't, that the roles had been reversed, Chauncey was mentally kneeling in front of me, the child, saying, "It's going to be okay."

Chauncey and I slowly worked our way back to *Bagan* and we joined the others back aboard. All were deep in their various pursuits and jobs. I was happy to hear Clinton down in the engine room and to see that Dominique was catching up on some much-needed sleep. Sefton was busy working at his music on his computer, and Greg was poised in the salon, ready for a shore trip of his own. Up until this point, Greg hadn't had a full, unfettered shore exploration where he could concentrate 100 percent on his photography. Right now the timing seemed perfect. Chauncey did a quick turnaround and the two of them headed back to the barren and steep-sided shore where Chauncey and I had recently had my venting session.

Time passed, the day rolled on, the sun started to set, and, for the first time in two months, we saw the moon, a ghost of a moon but one that was making itself known over the towering cliffs that held us firmly in the bay. We greeted the moon with great celebration. It was a small but important suggestion that we were starting to close in on a life we had left months earlier. Yet it also proved to be a sighting of the gravest concern for it meant that the days were decisively starting to get short and daylight needed to make precious miles was growing short. A squawk from the VHF interrupted my afternoon's reading. Chauncey was calling *Bagan* from shore with a none-too-subtle note of urgency in his voice. Greg had wandered off, leaving him alone on shore and without a gun, he reported. Had the steep, threatening, rocky gray cliffs which loomed so high over us suddenly collapsed around us, I could not have been more upset and concerned. Earlier in the day, we had seen a polar bear roaming far atop one of the cliffs and quickly his presence loomed large. I told Chauncey to come back to the boat immediately.

Coming aboard cold and shaken, Chauncey filled us in. They had both gotten ashore with no problem and once secured, Chauncey had set up the tripod and camera to do a self-interview, something that we were all working on—thoughts and reflections about the trip to date. About halfway through, Chauncey had looked up and saw that Greg was missing and had taken the rifle with him, leaving Chauncey at water's edge as night was falling and with absolutely no means of protecting himself.

Chauncey had spent the better part of thirty minutes calling Greg on their set of two-ways but to no avail. Thinking that perhaps his batteries might have died, he tried hollering for him, but still no Greg. Finally giving up and starting to feel every bit like the potential prey that he was, he contacted me. Greg's wandering had placed not only Chauncey but now himself in extreme danger. I told Chauncey he had done the right thing. Only a few hours earlier, I was expressing how sick of the trip I was. That was nothing compared to how I felt now.

I took Big Black and lazily drifted a few feet off the barren shore alone. The small, sharp rocks at water's edge didn't prove for the best of waiting spots so I floated in circles as I waited for Greg and rehearsed what I was going to say. I wanted to unload on him with everything I had. It was that sort of day that I wanted to unload on anyone with everything I had. Greg's leaving Chauncey alone and without a gun was completely and perhaps fatally unacceptable. My role called for dispassionately letting Greg know that this wandering off alone should never happen again.

With Greg now back aboard, we had a short meeting about the incident and Greg proved to be every bit the forthright and responsible man that I knew him to be. He offered no excuses. He clearly understood and accepted the situation that had occurred and freely admitted to what had happened shouldn't have and never would again. He allowed Chauncey to air his feelings and after the meeting they sealed their day with a hug. It was moments like this that gave me the energy and faith to continue with the trip. It's no exaggeration to say that by this point in the trip it was moments like these that gave me the strength to roll out of bed for each watch and face the latest less-than-good situation with energy. Life is life and as such will always be filled with issues and problems, but the very nature of what we were undertaking held far more problems than moments like these, so I knew I had to cling to what their hug did for the trip and myself.

Their talk also helped to push back some of the ever-present tension that had a few days ago started to slowly sneak back into things. Everybody was sick of the trip at this point, tired of the waiting and I'm sure had been running their own numbers as to how and when we'd get out. Clinton claimed that he was having the "time of his life" and if this consisted of cheap shots and sarcastic remarks at Dominique and Chauncey, I'm sure he was.

The underlying pressures were constant and there was no true getting away from them. They were a fact of life and we all had to adjust accordingly. So when moments of optimism and good news came, they were received with a note of celebration, which was grossly disproportionate to that of everyday life. These positive advances or developments would almost make me giddy—none more so than what Clinton shouted from the pilothouse that evening.

We were cleaning up after dinner, getting ready to fall into our sleeping bags to sleep or read and once again, rotate into our two-hour anchor watches. Clinton was in the pilothouse and was downloading the latest ice charts by himself. He saw it immediately, and let us all know what he saw in no uncertain terms, "WE... ARE... OUTTA... HERE!!"

The latest ice charts showed a definite lead opening up along the east side of the sound and the projections indicated it would be more in the hours and days to come.

The flood of happiness and relief that washed over me was nothing short of a reprieve from a death sentence. For many days, I'd been looking at the scenarios of turning back, if we could, perhaps leaving the boat in Cambridge Bay for the winter or, if worse came to worse, wintering over in the ice; all plans of action shifted to some of the darkest, most failure-ridden and personally unacceptable thinking into which I'd ever slid.

Clinton's news and our visual evidence suggested we were soon to be out of this neighborhood of ice traps, dead explorers, and sunken ships within the next twenty-four to thirty-six hours.

Were it only so.

CHAPTER 12

CRACKS IN THE ICE

"Have I brought my family together only to lead them to their deaths?" The thought screeched through my head over and over again as I tried to sleep.

How could I have been so stupid? How could I have not seen the big picture? Ours wasn't to be a trip of adventure, an eleventh-hour expedition that a family rallied around; it was a trip about death. I'd completely overlooked the obvious. There was a very real chance that we wouldn't make it out of our current situation and death was a constant.

We'd set off from Pasley Bay early in the morning with great optimism and enthusiasm. *Bagan* headed south into Peel Sound and as the ice charts showed us, the lead on the east side of the Sound was farther open and the trend appeared to be continuing. Almost two weeks of waiting was now paying off and if it continued as it had for the past twelve hours, we'd be in Gjoa Haven, a short stop before Cambridge Bay, in a few short days.

It was a cloudless, blue-sky day with little wind and the Sound was glass-flat. Temperatures hovered in the low thirties and for now, the nagging problem of the small hydraulic pump hadn't been in evidence. While waiting in Pasley Bay, Clinton had made some calls and found the post office wouldn't forward the package from Resolute onto Cambridge Bay for us. For now, the pump was quiet and we didn't need the stabilizers but as with so many things on the trip, it was only a matter of time.

Heading down to the lead in the ice, *Bagan* passed through some of the most spectacular scenery any of us had ever witnessed. At one point, we threaded our way past the Tasmania Islands, a small outcropping of low-lying, ragged rock islands bordered to the west by a spectacularly large black and gray cliff covered by perhaps thousands of white terns. While these terns were nesting, swooping, darting into and out of the water, deep blue ice sheets were being swept by to the south, occasionally catching on the smaller islets and by force of the current, slowly bunching up and occasionally exploding, shattering from the building force of the pressure of the currents against the rocks. It was a spectaular day to be alive and in the Northwest Passage.

From the pilothouse, Clinton and I inched *Bagan* into the dangerous grouping of islands.

The current was pushing us along at two knots over the bottom, and to have any steering we needed to go at least another two knots. The view was spectacular, but the dangerous and exhilarating ride turned very suddenly against us. An eddy boosted our over-the-ground-speed to five knots and was pushing us directly to a sharp-pointed, north-facing ledge upon which ice sheets up to two-feet thick were piling up against and exploding upon.

"We're bailing out," Clinton shouted. If we stayed on this course, we'd be pushed onto the rocks. We made a ninety-degree turn and poured it on, narrowly slipping by and avoiding a crash. We felt comfortable and confident with our instantaneous decision and ship handling. As we collectively released our breaths, we had no way of realizing that our real problems were just beginning.

Bagan continued south dodging ice floes and managing to get deeper into the ice sheet. At approximately 11 a.m., I relieved Clinton. Chauncey, Dominique, and I sat in the pilothouse continuing on our slow, zigzag path south. Perhaps five miles to the south, it looked as though the light was play-ing a trick of refraction on us. The height of sea level seemed doubled on the horizon. This trick of the eye was something we had seen from time to time on the trip and at that point had no reason to think differently. Yet as we closed in, it seemed all too real. On radar and through the binoculars, we saw we were quickly approaching the leading north edge of an ice sheet that ex-tended across Peel Sound to the west as far as the eye could see.

In mere minutes, we were upon this frozen ragged barrier and no lead or opening was evident. Maybe we had gone too far west to find the lead. We altered course and ran along this icy edge, following it to the east, closer to shore. No lead. We reversed course and now ran back to the west, looking for the lead that last night and this morning's ice charts showed. By this time, we'd had to throttle back due to some offerings of tightly packed ice groups several times; the adjustment in RPMs was enough to wake Clinton up. As we all did when we'd hear *Bagan*'s large Lugger engine spool down, he quick-ly came up to the pilothouse, took one look at the impenetrable sheet in front of us, and demanded, "What the fuck did you guys do?"

Not exactly the sort of question I wanted to hear right then but one that deserved no energy in the way of a response for as each foot we traveled things started to look increasingly grim.

We flowed along the north end of the ice pack for perhaps another twenty minutes all the while looking for the lead we so clearly saw in the last two ice charts. It simply wasn't there. Clinton and I conferred and decided to head back to our previous anchorage and regroup, think about our next step and what may have possibly gone wrong in our current one.

No sooner had we turned *Bagan* north than what we saw ahead of us was sobering and frightening: what appeared to be an ice sheet every bit as substantial as the one we were now heading away from was pressing down from the north. Clinton quickly got online and found the latest ice charts. There was no lead, we were very nearly trapped. Our previous anchorage, Pasley Bay, was now iced in. Had we stayed there another day, we wouldn't have gotten out.

Our options, such as they were, were dwindling. With both sheets of ice coming together, about the only thing we could do to improve our current situation was to try to push our way into and through the southern ice. At least we'd be moving with it and not trying to fight through it against a countercurrent.

We'd proceed into an opening, go as far as we could, try to find another opening and regardless the size, work our way into it and try to get some further distance south. While the first few hours of this routine gave us some much needed optimism, it wasn't to last. By the second hour of this, we had all settled into our various roles and for the next sixteen hours never left our respective stations. Clinton was atop the radar arch with binoculars trying to find possible leads, anywhere from ten- to twenty-feet wide. If he found one, he'd call me in the pilothouse and give me the bearing for the next lead as well as the lead after that. "In fifty feet you'll want to turn twenty degrees to starboard and enter what looks like a small dogleg going off to the west. Once through, look for another small open bearing about thirty degrees to port." I was inside at the helm trying to watch the radar and depth sounder, and following Clinton's directions. As we'd approach these small openings, Sefton was at the bow with the laminated pole for the underwater camera rig, using it to push us off any underwater shelf we couldn't see which could threaten to rip into *Bagan*'s hull. What seemed like thousands of times that day, I'd hear Sefton on the deck speaker calling out, "Twenty feet, ten feet, five feet, about to hit... Indeed we have!" Once a gentle and controlled contact was made with a piece of ice (ranging in size from two feet to 100 feet), I'd have to do the unthinkable and use *Bagan* as an icebreaker. If our forward momentum failed, I'd have to slowly get her into neutral and then back up and try from another angle. Dominique and Greg were stationed on the stern with their one set of two-way radios and would warn me if backing up was even possible, since ice was constantly threatening to go under our stern and get into our prop.

Even the lightest of dings on the prop would have caused trip-ending damage. Chauncey worked the side decks and would try to pole ice away from *Bagan* where it, too, was threatening to go under her sides and damage the stabilizers. And, when he wasn't fending off of ice, he was filming and getting some of the most spectacular footage I'd ever seen. It was breathtaking in its simplicity and heartbreaking in its depiction of a day of diminishing options.

As we tried to work our way south, we would be happy with a hundred yards gained. Over the next sixteen hours we lowered our expectations and hopes from a hundred yards to fifty yards to a hundred feet to fifty feet all the way down to a matter of mere inches.

On August 16, at 2 a.m. *Bagan* officially stopped making forward progress. We were hopelessly trapped, unable to make even an inch forward, backwards, or sideways. We were locked in with a haunting and deathly encompassing fog and had completely and decisively run out of options. Ironically, despite our array of modern day electronics and safety devices we were no better off than those who went and died before us and could do nothing about it. The ice had caught us and we had lost.

"Have I brought my family together only to lead them to their deaths?" I wondered.

While the past eighteen hours were filled with physical and navigational challenges, the mental toll was also brutal. Although fairly recent cruisers had done The Passage over several seasons with seemingly no concern or fears, I found my experience to be the complete opposite. The myriad pre-trip pressures—losing funding, the personality conflicts, my health issues, the documentary, and now the responsibility of my kids' lives—it was almost more than I could handle. Reading other reports of previous transits, I found my experience was entirely different because few of these books or articles mentioned the deep and raging fear that could start and grow inside of you.

Perhaps I wasn't the sort who should have taken on such a demanding trip.

Was I scared? I don't know. None of these concerns were ever paralyzing, but they loomed large mentally, and I felt it best not to burden anyone around me.

When we had entered the ice, I was still being plagued by the black thoughts of how the trip could potentially end. Fears and fatigue showed no limits to their depths and, as each futile hour ticked by, the sounds and experiences became more frightening. At first I thought that the great creaks, moans, and explosions I could hear from deep inside *Bagan* were her hull, her structure being overcome by the icy and deadly pressures. With each deep and rumbling snap I heard, I could "see" damage being done below the water line. At one point, I called Sefton into the pilothouse and quietly asked him to go below and pull some floorboards because I feared we had compromised the hull. After a few minutes below, Sefton found that the bilges were as dry as the day we left Newport, then headed back outside into the sharp Arctic air to continue fending ice off the bow. I'd be relieved momentarily, until the next groan and explosion told me that what I'd been listening to was the massive amounts of thick ice giving way with great protestations as *Bagan* gained another two or three feet.

At various times during that first day, we lost power in the bow thruster, lost two push poles, several sets of gloves, and a two-way radio over the side only to watch them get swallowed up in a matter of seconds by the ice. *Bagan* and crew became a floating, small island of survival that at any moment could be broached, and if past history had anything to do with it, could be snuffed out and ground into the bottom in a heartbeat. These were my most fearful of thoughts, not based entirely in reality but by the same token entirely possible. They didn't rule my thinking for the next few days but did manage to lower the bar of my experience; "Who the hell were we, was I, to think we could take on a transit in a part of the Arctic which had claimed so many hundreds of lives before?"

The audacity and seeming hubris of undertaking such a project gained a loud and unrelenting voice inside of me, one that I had to constantly struggle with and try to keep in check for had the others gotten a whiff of these fears and insecurities, I felt it would be detrimental to keeping their own fears at bay. It was a constant balance of letting them know that I felt our situation to be extremely difficult but not deadly. That first night of being held captive in the Arctic ice was brutal. That night potential headlines ran through my head: "Father Leads Family To Icy Death," "Half-assed Explorer Loses Not Only Funding But Boat As Well."

By 2:30 a.m., we had dropped two anchors on the ice and had all tried to roll-in and gain what rest we could, knowing that thinking of sleep was more a joke than a wish. After a few fraught-filled hours of total disbelief of where we now found ourselves, I ambled up to the salon for tea and was immediately accosted by Greg. He and Chauncey had been up for a while and had worked out a few "photo-ops" which they were anxious to start in on. Greg's enthusiasm was a great indication that they perhaps had been spared some of my darker thoughts, but was also a bit ill-timed. "Got a question for you; Chauncey and I want to go out onto the ice and get some shots and then I'm going to dive under the ice to get some footage. Where's the underwater housing?" Having just spent hours trying to keep the ice at bay, I failed to immediately share in Greg's pressing enthusiasm and quickly answered, "No one's going anywhere as I don't trust the ice. No!" I thought about it a bit more and then offered up, "If you do this, you're going to sign waivers as I'm not going to be held responsible for you." While I trusted the crew's intent, aim, and honesty, it was the liability factor from those they left behind that loomed large before me.

In my mind's eye, I was thinking back onto the polar bear we saw on the ice outside of Resolute Bay and how quickly and with great stealth he managed to maneuver into and around the ice floes. I continued, "Jesus, Greg..." and stopped, for far as the eye could see, we were locked into the ice and the thought of these two guys going out onto and under it didn't sit too well with me.

Chauncey, being an individual who could always quickly sum up and deal with most any situation, held the key to my cooperation and acquiescence to their plan for the morning.

"Sprague," he asked as he came up to me, "do you need a hug?" and with that gave me a manly hug and a reassuring pat on the back and told me to sit down and he'd fix up a hot mug of black tea for me. My stepson had hit the nail on the head; I needed to wake up, have some heavy-duty caffeine and a hug of reassurance that while yesterday's horrors did indeed happen, there was much to be gained in our current position.

Again, Chauncey proved to be a man wise beyond his years.

With mug of hot tea in hand, I wandered out onto the foredeck, to take in all that surrounded us. Ice and barren land definitely, but the power and beauty of what I beheld overpowered, if only for a few minutes, the deep concerns and fears I nursed for the past few days. From the magnificent shapes, muted colors, and abstract designs of the low barren hills to the twisted beauty of the menacing ice sheets, Mother Nature was on full display and for that briefest of moments, I realized that we were some of the luckiest people on earth. I was presently surrounded by some of the planet's rawest beauty, something that very few would be able to ever see. Albeit stuck, we had indeed made it this far into a land of powerful and abject beauty. In that spot, at that time, I could not have been happier, more elated. An explosive shattering of ice in the distance broke my revelry and quickly brought me back to the reality at hand.

With Greg's help, Chauncey had gotten into his survival suit, attached to a 100-foot climbing line, and was making his way off onto the ice floes, getting remarkable shots of a trapped *Bagan*. We had set up a man on the radar arch with a rifle and glasses to keep bear-watch for him, and Chauncey managed to get remarkable stills and HD video of never-before-seen footage. Shortly after Chauncey's testing of the ice, one by one we all made it out onto the solid floes and began to inspect *Bagan* for what I was sure was extreme damage from the previous days. As I walked around the ice pressing in on her hull I was becoming astonished and at one point simply refused to believe what I was seeing. Through all the horrendous abuse we had put her through, despite having to ask the unthinkable of her and use her to batter her way through, she only suffered one ding on her bow bulb, five inches long and maybe three-quarters of an inch deep. There had to have been more to it than that and shortly after Chauncey came back on board, we sent Greg over the side with underwater camera gear and another 100-foot tether.

Before he went over, we set down some very strict ground rules: no deeper than twenty feet and do not venture out of sight under the ice sheets. He came back with breathtaking footage. When he surfaced after his first fifteen-minute submersion, which included a thorough inspection of our hull, he came to the surface shaking his head. My heart sank and I expected the worst.

Removing his full-face mask he continued to shake his head saying, "Not a scratch, nothing. Apart from the ding on the bow, nothing." Only a Nordhavn could have taken such abusive treatment and come out of it shining.

We decided to sit tight for a few more hours, and after trying to get some rest, hopefully look at things with a new perspective.

The night before we were a mile and a half off shore. Due to unseen current we now found ourselves a quarter mile off shore. It wasn't hard to see the fate of the ice arriving at these large jagged, brown, and mottled rocks before us. The ice would slowly lean, press up against it, and after enough pressure had built up, explode and shatter onto the barren and ragged beach. If we couldn't act quickly, in two hours we'd end up doing the same. By this time, all but Clinton had gathered in the pilothouse to take in the situation. I went below, told Clinton we had a decision to make and asked him to come up and join us. We were facing black and white, sink or not sink, be ground into the rocks ahead of us or somehow maneuver *Bagan* so she was facing west and try to ram our way away from the beach.

The bright blue-sky day had had some small effect on the ice pressing in around us and some small pockets of water had opened. Whether they were deep enough to accommodate *Bagan*'s six-foot draft was another thing. We desperately needed to get *Bagan* far enough west to secure us some distance and time from being crushed on shore, regardless of the outcome in the ice which was waiting for us.

We fired up *Bagan*'s engine and hoped for the best. I had no idea the outcome, but knew that if she were to go down, I'd rather have her sink trying to claw her way away from the rocks and go down fighting than succumb to a brutal and inglorious end.

Again we used *Bagan* as an icebreaker, hooking her bulbous bow under sheets of ice and pouring on the coals as grinding and exploding ice all around us reminded me of what was at stake. At times her bow would ride up and on top of the ice only to break the sheet into halves all the while gaining perhaps another three feet.

We backed and filled, rammed and pushed, again and again pushing her to the limits of her ability. Again the bow thruster quit on us and at one point I saw Big Black pass us on the ice out the starboard side. For hours, we listened to the shrieking and groaning of the ice around us as *Bagan*'s engine would beef up her RPMs and then quickly drop back; sometimes having an immediate effect, sometimes setting into motion a chain reaction which had an almost imperceptible effect on ice 500 yards away.

It was grueling and torturous work that pushed us all beyond our limits. Tempers were short and time was running out. At one point, from his station on the radar arch, Clinton was trying to advise me of the next potential ten-foot lead when the small two-way radio he was using crapped out. In utter frustration, he tossed the radio down onto the boat deck, shattering it into pieces. We had been working at our effort for more than twelve hours and only managed four miles.

By 11 p.m., I could literally not see straight. For more than twelve straight hours we'd all been on our feet, physically and mentally seeking answers where none were to be found. My toe was on fire, sending shock waves of pain up into my leg. I asked Clinton to take the wheel for me while I worked a side deck and Chauncey replaced him on the radar arch. Clinton found a fairly open lead, gained a remarkable 100 yards and then once again became trapped. He called up to Chauncey for a suggestion and only by bad luck of the draw, Chauncey sent us down into an ice-choked dead end. Clinton shorted out. Without waiting for *Bagan*'s engine to slow its forward spin, he slammed her into reverse and blasted out of the trap backwards saying, "That asshole. I oughta go up there and kick his ass!"

Chauncey came down from the radar arch. He took me aside and strongly requested that I get back on the helm. I couldn't. Mentally I had absolutely nothing left. Physically I couldn't take anymore. I told Clinton to find a thick sheet and drop the anchors so we could get some rest. We'd gained four miles and I didn't want to give up an inch.

I crawled into my sleeping bag and I heard the anchor drop and set on the ice. I heard Greg walk a second anchor out as a backup.

Silence.

A few small nervous laughs from above and soon all were in their bunks, hopefully sleeping. By this time, sleep was completely out of the picture for me and I knew I had to concentrate on simply resting. My mind was a random clutter of odds and ends, none of which were pertinent now or made any sense—a kaleidoscope of scenes and sounds from my youth, twelve-meter racing, college memories, the trip, a past car accident, a second grade play. There was no logic to them and there was no controlling them. For the second time we had simply and completely run out of options and our fate was at the hands of whatever it is that guides us. I'm sure that had I been dropped into this scenario, helicoptered in from "civilization," all would be fairly straightforward and manageable.

By this time, the trip had taken such a mental and physical toll that I now realized I had long since run out of the energy it takes to put on a "smiling face." The pain in my foot was excruciating, the touch of the sleeping bag exacerbating an already torturous feeling. Every nerve in my foot felt as if it were on fire. The pressure of a sock was out of the question. The stress alone of leading my children into a situation that held very little evidence for a good outcome had pushed me into a place that was blacker and deeper than I ever knew existed. I hadn't given up and certainly wouldn't do so, but by the same token I knew I held no more answers and didn't have the strength required to put on a front that would suggest that I did.

I lay in my bunk, thinking, meditating, and praying to anyone and everyone who'd listen. I was bargaining with all things of nature and spiritual and offered up that I would take any route, rise to any challenge, or make any sacrifice so that the kids remained safe. In the silence, I could hear the ice shifting, groaning, pressing, and slowly sliding past the hull. Far-off explosions from deep below us constantly reminded me that as I lay there, seeking answers, Mother Nature was at work and the clock was ticking.

I tried to concentrate on breathing, counting and feeling the breaths in and out, my heart beats the same. The voices from the dark place wondered where these breaths and beats came from, if there was any guarantee that there would be one after this? How was I sure that this system would work every time one beat ended or my lungs emptied the current breath and sought another one? Who commanded the next one and was I sure that there'd be one? It wasn't a fixation nor was it a panic; it was a question for all that I'd previously assumed. I didn't conjure it up but in the face of our current predicament, it demanded these answers of me.

I'd love to say that it was enlightening but it wasn't. These were as deeply disturbing questions as I'd ever faced and when I pulled myself from them, I found my icy and indifferent surroundings offered no comfort with equally disturbing questions of their own.

At some point, I must have fallen asleep for from a place far away from the Arctic nightmare we were now in, I felt Chauncey shaking me.

"Wake up... Sprague... wake up! We're out... we're seven miles down the coast." Somehow I was able to hear what he said and able to lock onto it but was pretty sure it was part of the dream state I felt I was still in. "Out of the ice???" I asked. "No, still in the ice but seven miles away from land and into Peel Sound." And with that he dashed back to up to the pilothouse.

I was awake and I'd heard what I heard. We were no longer heading for the rocks but while still jammed in the ice, it appeared as though we'd been given some breathing room and by whatever means were now seven miles away from the potential crushing destruction on the rocks ashore and in the open.

This all flooded over me in a wave of emotion I can't remember experiencing. I wept uncontrollably, releasing all the pressures and tensions of the past week and now, finally, I was able to grab an emotional breath I didn't know I needed. I don't know what lay ahead in the next minute, hour, or day, but I knew that for now we were handed a very simple and straightforward chance.

CHAPTER 13

BAGAN BREAKS FREE

"Thank you for the best day of my life!"

As I was sitting in the helm seat, reflecting back on the past 48 hours of sheer hell, Chauncey had come up from the galley with a mug of black tea and handed it to me.

"It was the best day of my life because we escaped and it was the best day because nothing could compare to what we just survived."

Earlier in the afternoon, the ice began to slowly dissipate, leads became longer, and there was more room for maneuverability. Our freedom played out in reverse of our entrapment; where we'd fight for a few inches now turned into feet, then yards. We were still dodging ice floes, but with a slight deviation to course, they weren't presenting the threat or finality they had for the past two harrowing days. My mental disposition was far better than it had been, and I could again concentrate on the task at hand without the relentless weight of "what-ifs."

As Chauncey and I sat and talked, I knew that having opened up that area of sheer desperation, loneliness, and fear, it would always be present to one degree or another. It had decreased in volume, but I knew it was always lurking. The rest of the trip was going to be single focus, a simple job—a very demanding and exhausting job but as the last few moments showed a richly rewarding one as well.

"Were you scared?" I asked Chauncey. He took a minute to think, looked about at the remains of the ice and making direct and no uncertain eye contact offered back, "I was, but always knew we'd get out either on land or by boat. I never doubted."

I was hoping that I had something to do with his confidence but ultimately was very happy to know that our predicament hadn't gotten the better of him and commanded his imagination. He continued, "You must be beat."

I chuckled. It would have been a full laugh but found I didn't have the energy. "Yeah, I am, all I could do was think about you guys." At one point during the battle, I lay down in my bunk, tried to force my thoughts back onto open green fields, spring flowers, babies laughing, anything but the continuous cacophony of the endless megatons of indifferent ice sheets pressing in on us. At one point, the horrific protests of the ice floes, the deadly earnestness with which they jammed up against one another with banshee's screams, had me thinking I'd put on a pair of headphones and listen to music, hoping that that could take my mind off obsessing about the futile. But I didn't. While it might take me to another, happier, and more tranquil place, I feared what would happen when the music stopped. Would I be able to make the re-entry into the demanding and hopelessly realistic world of the Arctic in one mental piece?

Clinton and I had taken some time to pore over the charts and look at our next option. The next planned stop was Gjoa Haven, an Inuit community of perhaps 900 people, where we could stop for a day and catch our breaths before we headed farther south and west to Cambridge Bay. It was in Gjoa Haven that Roald Amundsen stayed two winters in the middle of his attempt to transit the Northwest Passage.

His transit quest took him from 1903-06 and it was from this tiny hamlet that he set out on the final leg of his historic trip. Amundsen was the first to make the passage and our stopping in his final staging area seemed not only appropriate but also timely.

Being relatively ice-free now, something none of us will ever again take for granted, we cautiously and slowly powered through the small window of night and arrived in Gjoa Haven at 2:45 a.m. on August 19. Quietly and with a well-practiced drill in the dark of an Arctic night, we dropped the anchor in the town's outer bay and, forgoing the usual anchor watch, we all found sleep.

The events of the past few days still weighed heavily, enough that when we finally did awaken, there wasn't the usual morning chatter. I think we were all shell-shocked. It was going to take a long time to digest what we had survived, something I knew I'd be dealing with for years.

Shortly, two shore parties were formed and while Chauncey, Sefton, and I went off to film some of the area, the others went into town to do what food shopping they could. To this day, I'm not exactly sure how it happened but Dominique, Greg, and Clinton ended up in the mayor's office and were given the official welcome to Gjoa Haven—plus an official coffee mug, pens, and pins. Knowing that *Bagan* was perhaps the third boat they'd seen all year, we realized that the mayor was as delighted with our visit as we were with his welcome.

It had been over a month since we had seen another person or boat, and the feeling of wandering around the small, empty town was similar to the feeling I'd get in Manhattan, bustling and noisy. With low, dirt-brown hills and a smattering of trailers, Gjoa Haven reflected the rugged life found in that part of the Northwest Passage. Dirt streets, caribou hides being cured, sled dogs straining, yelping, tugging at their chains as we'd walk past. The sudden arrival of an ATV had me jumping out of my shoes and when approached by a stranger, I found I was flooded with a warmth of joy.

Never quite drawn to people or groups of them, I found that I was the sort who came away drained and not recharged from parties. One-on-one contact was about all I could handle.

And while one month of isolation and desolation didn't show me the light and turn me into a gregarious creature, it did spell out that man is a social animal and that as much as I insisted to the contrary, I needed human contact and social interaction in my life. Standing on the shore of Gjoa Haven, discussing last season's fishing or a particular winter of twenty years ago was about as sweet as it got. I found myself listening to nothing in particular, everything in general and with the feeling of, "Just keep talking!"

Late in the evening of the first day at Gjoa Haven, Clinton and I once again downloaded charts and saw that while the ice was going to give us a break, at least for now, two small depressions in the Chukchi Sea were forming and heading to the east. The predicted winds weren't anything we couldn't deal with, perhaps twenty-five knots at best, but because of what we had just come out of, we decided to up-anchor and head west to McClintock Bay, which was tucked into the west side of Simpson Strait, a narrow and steep-sided passage on the south side of King William Island. Our original plan was to go through the strait, then on the west side of the island, turn north and head for the northwest corner, an area where Franklin's two ships, the *Erebus* and *Terror,* were thought to have vanished.

Where, how, and why they vanished isn't known and perhaps never will be, but from the few artifacts and bones found over the years, it is generally felt this northwest corner was about as far as they got. We found we were still exhausted, the weather was potentially dicey, and that we had a new and deep respect for the potential of ice.

And the charts for that side of King William Island were remarkably inadequate. Where nautical charts will show numbers representing bottom depths by the thousands, this full chart had one tiny set of numbers, more an ant trail than anything, that were entered in the mid-1800s. Discretion ruled out and after two fog-bound days, *Bagan* dropped the hook in McClintock Bay where we stayed for the next 48 hours. The bay was named for Sir Francis McClintock who, in 1859, on the northwest corner of King William Island, found grizzly evidence of the lost Franklin expedition and reported back to a not-very-understanding Victorian England that theirs was a tragic demise which ended in, among other things, cannibalism.

Wherever we went aboard *Bagan*, no matter the size or shape of the bay or anchorage, history was always present.

Those that went before us, if they did survive and escape The Passage, returned with facts of brutal and untimely deaths and destruction by swift and impersonal natural forces. Those facts were now haunting each of us.

The first evening in McClintock Bay proved wilder than predicted, with biting winds that roared in off the flat and gray Arctic surroundings. Most breezes offer an exhilarating feeling, something that piques the challenge of romance or adventure in you. These winds were anything but and the clear message we received from them was the same as we experienced in Griffin Inlet: "You are not wanted here and we offer no comfort. Move on."

It was a feeling that was becoming increasingly palpable as we downloaded weather charts for the next few days. While we weren't facing any immediate threat, the beginnings of winter were making themselves known in Siberia and it was understood that our relative days of ease were coming to an end. Late in the day, Chauncey, Greg, Sefton, Dominique, and I took to the shore to film and stretch our legs as the wind howled and pockets of dark, black moisture-laden clouds scudded over us. I well remember the feeling in an otherwise bright blue-sky day that on August 21, summer was over, that we had wasted valuable time waiting as winter was coming on early. For once the low pressures started to develop and roll out of Siberia they'd do so with more and more regularity and continue to build to unimaginable proportions.

With this in mind, we decided that evening over a wonderful meal of hamburgers, and fresh salad to celebrate Greg's birthday. Then we decided to head for Cambridge Bay, where we wanted to take on much-needed fuel. Getting through the ice had burned much more than expected. Clinton and I had originally estimated that we'd come into Cambridge Bay with approximately 300 gallons in reserve. The actual fact of the matter was we had just about less than 100 gallons. Again something I chose not to share with the rest of the crew. We also desperately needed gas for Big Black.

The two-day hop to Cambridge Bay was about as straightforward as it could be and by this time we'd become used to incomplete charts, total immersion in pea-soup fog, and the occasional and unexpected floes of stray ice and snow. I don't think that it was a matter of actually being used to it as much as it was a sense that despite the rest at Gjoa Haven, we were all running through our mental reserves. It would take weeks if not months to get us all back to where we were before we left Newport. Whatever the step after running on adrenalin is, that is where we all now found ourselves; a condition whose disturbing depths would play out repeatedly, but never like what happened on the foredeck of *Bagan* a day out of Cambridge Bay.

The day had been about as normal as one could have hoped for, dense fog followed by brilliant sunlight, clear waters then small, threatening pockets of ice, a well-behaved engine room then the gut-wrenching racket from the hydraulic pump; nothing we couldn't deal with yet never truly being able to relax. I was at the helm and Sefton was on the foredeck doing ice watch. Dominique, Greg, and Clinton were either sleeping or reading. Sefton and I were able to communicate over a two-way external speaker on the foredeck, one that would not only broadcast your voice through a hand-held microphone from inside, but would also pick up sounds and conversations from the foredeck and broadcast them back into the pilothouse.

All was relatively fine, Sefton and I each watching, helping *Bagan* make some good progress west. At one point, Chauncey joined Sefton on the foredeck and their usual wonderful banter started, laughter. I heard Chauncey say something to the effect that the foredeck was littered with line and a pole and that Sefton should clean it up. Normally not an overt statement but these were far from normal times. Sefton offered back that it was fine as is and not to worry about it. Chauncey took it a step further and told Sefton to clean it up. Sefton is a very low-key guy and unless truly pushed handles most situations in stride. Seeming to want to put an end to the discussion, Sefton told Chauncey he'd clean it up in due time. I can't remember the exact words but this was unacceptable to Chauncey and the flame of the match was getting dangerously close to the fuse. It escalated further until I heard

Sefton say as he stared Chauncey down, "Well then let's settle this here and now. Let's go for it." In the few seconds that they remained eye-locked, I had to make a decision. Do I intervene? Should I call one of them in off the foredeck on a false pretense? Should I ignore it and let the sibling tension run itself out or was this something which could escalate quickly? It dawned on me then how little I knew about each of them. As much as the trip had brought us closer together and allowed the barrier of hurt and distance to subside, I felt that I didn't know whom each of them was underneath it all and I certainly didn't know in what conditions the past week or so had left them. As trip leader, do I let them blow off steam and, if worse came to worse, allow punches to be thrown? As a parent, do I get in the middle of something that may have had a history that went much further back than simply the last two months? The hardest thing to do was to not react and yet that's exactly what I found myself doing; they weren't little boys but young men who were making their way in life and as such were in need of defining who they were and what they stood for.

I sat and watched as they slowly dropped eye contact and Chauncey walked off the foredeck: no winner or loser, simply two strong-minded individuals who backed off from a situation that defined borders and personalities. It wasn't more than a few hours later Chauncey came back, sat down beside Sefton who was still on the foredeck, and quietly apologized. No great moment of mea culpa, no great admission of lack of sensitivity or for that matter nothing especially in the way of a great acquiescence. Chauncey hooked his arm around Sefton's neck and said that he was out of place.

Sefton answered Chauncey's admission with, "Cool." And once again all was as it was, easy as that. I can't ever remember being more proud of two individuals for whom I held so much love.

On August 23, with one eye on the weather and one eye on the dwindling fuel reserves, we arrived in Cambridge Bay at 8:15 a.m. and, after several nights of running in the fog and dodging ice floes with now four hours of darkness, we pushed to get the needed chores done before we all set about trying to gain back some sleep.

Cambridge Bay is an Inuit community of approximately 1,500. What struck me immediately about the town was that because of permafrost, the homes were all built above ground.

When it came to matters of global warming, who better to interview than these residents of this town that was truly at Ground Zero. Some streets were paved; others for the most part were dry, swirling dust and dirt. To the untrained eye, Cambridge Bay seemed as remote and barren as other anchorages we'd visited in the past month. But upon a closer look, the town showed itself to be a thriving town with a wonderful mixture of modern technology and Inuit tradition. Some trucks, more ATVs, many wooden sleds up for the summer season and smiles by the dozen. Wherever we went, we were met with a wonderful combination of welcome and great curiosity. There were two people in particular who welcomed us to town with the hospitality and warmth one would expect from some of the southern states in the U.S.: Peter Semotiuk, our ice guru, and Vicki Aitaok, who ran the town's visitors' center. Vicki was to help with my interviews with elders and youngsters for my future documentary.

One of my first priorities was to touch base with both of these people and arrange to meet, but first, *Bagan* took on 1,850 gallons of desperately needed fuel—she holds 2,000. Dominique once again set to rotating food, Clinton started in on fluid changes in the engine room, and Greg, Chauncey, and Sefton started in on the much-needed and oft-disliked job of getting decks and topsides back to a decent state. In the middle of the flurry of cleaning and fueling, a very large, unimposing, and smiling man knocked on the hull.

I knew this had to be Peter. Welcoming him aboard, we found a place for him to sit and immediately all action stopped and everyone gathered. The salon was filled with laughter, something that had not been in evidence for quite a while. We peppered him with questions regarding winters in this desolate area.

Very quickly we learned from Peter that Cambridge Bay was like any other small community. While tight, it did offer the standard fare of PTA meetings, after-school clubs, and a Chamber of Commerce. Peter's presence aboard *Bagan* was one of the true lights of optimism and encouragement which we hadn't felt aboard for far too long. His knowledge of the Arctic and ice was a comfort to our rattled nerves.

After placing a few phone calls, I tracked down Vicki, who swung by in her truck and gave me a personal tour of town. She had arranged interviews, took me to meet my subjects, and we ended with a cup of tea at her home, where I met her husband, Jorgen, and the kids, who needed to be driven to basketball practice. Vicki was asking Jorgen what he had planned for the weekend. And if anyone was going to the supermarket, bread was needed. Living in such a remote and isolating area did present special demands: above-ground septic tanks, twenty-four–hour darkness, and plane trips to shop or play a basketball game.

And clearly, this content family wouldn't have it any other way.

When Vicki dropped me off, the fuel truck had gone, all cleaning equipment had been tucked away, and *Bagan* was looking better than ever. I gladly swapped out places with the others as they hiked the short distance into town to try to pick up the Wi-Fi signal from the local high school, where the next day we would be treated to a wonderful exhibition of Arctic sports and games: knuckle-hopping, leg-wrestling, and my all-time favorite that calls for two people sitting side-by-side to put one arm around the other, place a finger in the other's mouth, and pull for all it is worth.

Later on our first day, *Bagan* became a participant in a very unofficial game for the younger kids, a game that delighted them but concerned me: rock throwing. *Bagan* presented a wonderful target for baseball-sized rocks and after a few innings, we all decided that anchoring out in the bay, closer to the wreck of Amundsen's *Maud,* was safer.

The *Maud,* named for Queen Maud of Norway, and Amundsen's ship for his second expedition to the Arctic, was sold to the Hudson Bay Company in 1925 and lived out her days in Cambridge Bay. What's left of her rests at the bottom of the northeast section of the bay and while we never received a permit to dive and film on her, we did take advantage of some remarkable evening sun and filmed her from the water. Her bleached bones and rusted chainplates were framed beautifully against the vast, open, and barren hills of Victoria Island.

Cambridge Bay was our first real time spent back in civilization in more than eight weeks and as hard as it was to think about the next few legs, the weather charts were continuing to show us a subtle but recognizable trend: winter storms were becoming more organized and frequent. While they didn't present anything we couldn't deal with, there was a clear but small pattern. Summer had definitely come to an end and another savage winter was soon to be upon us.

We needed to get going.

At 4 a.m. on August 26, we left Cambridge Bay and headed for the 130th meridian, our unofficial official exit from the Northwest Passage. This imaginary line was perhaps three days away and it was all I could do to keep from fixating on it, wondering how I would feel if we managed to actually cross it, whom I would email and whom would I call? I tried to keep as busy as possible, writing articles, reviewing shot-sheets for the documentary with Chauncey, fashioning some sort of script, sending emails to various cable and network concerns to introduce the trip, and studying ice and weather charts.

About 36 hours after we left Cambridge Bay, we ran into the first of the two small depressions that were running ahead of schedule. Trying to power into thirty-five–knot west winds and with a countercurrent, we'd had just about enough of the pounding when Dominique and Sefton came up with a perfect anchorage. Summer's Harbor, just south of Victoria Island, and slightly east of the Dolphin and Union Strait, was a perfect-shaped horse-shoe anchorage to protect us from the mounting gales that swept over us in succession.

Its flat, barren, gray, and rocky profile protected us as we watched the gales roll by outside of the small harbor. Nothing was required of us for the few days we were there, but I marveled at how, despite the rest in Cambridge Bay, we had fallen back to that state of exhaustion. Silence reigned, inter-rupted by the occasional sarcastic comment couched in anxiety and fatigue.

After the promised break, we once again headed *Bagan* west. Snow flurries came and went as we powered into the usual slop left over from the blow, something *Bagan* clearly took in stride.

By now the hydraulic pump had started to screech more loudly so we turned the stabilizers off and Clinton had called ahead to arrange to have yet another pump sent in to Barrow, Alaska, perhaps four days down the road. While I'd find it hard to say that all aboard *Bagan* were again under control, it was manageable, which under those conditions and that length of time underway, was about as good as it could get.

At 1:35 p.m. on August 30, we crossed the 130th meridian. We had transited the Northwest Passage.

Dominique created a "Bake-less Alaska" and we celebrated. We smiled, hugged, waved flags, and released great sighs of relief. We achieved what so many had failed, and died trying to do.

I was overwhelmed with memories of the Franklin Expedition, how 129 men gave their lives to do what we'd just accomplished. There's no comparison, they were supermen, heroes of their day, and honored explorers. While we did transit almost the same track, we had nearly unlimited electronic advantages plus charts and various comforts of home. While I don't try to fool myself into thinking we were anywhere near the level of those who went before us, there wasn't any denying we had completed the Northwest Passage in one season, a personal goal for more than half my lifetime.

I went up to the boat deck to try to come to terms with the past few months. With a few blatant exceptions, the crew had performed flawlessly. I felt a large wave of joy and pride push its way up through the exhaustion, mental fatigue, and lurking fear.

Bagan was now one of the handful of boats that history has seen and transited this Arctic Grail, yet better, far better than that was the fact that she did it with a family that fifteen years earlier had separated with no promise of reuniting.

To accomplish this, I had to recognize and depend on the strengths of a small crew that included my stepson, my stepdaughter, and my son, something that only three months ago I would never have considered as even remotely possible. Our relationships had started to grow and as we exited The Passage, I found that I held a love and concern for these children that I never before thought possible.

They all rose to the occasion, consistently countering frustration and exhaustion with respect and professionalism.

I couldn't have been prouder at what this journey had given me: a family.

Yet as overwhelming as this accomplishment was, a voice from within also went out on a limb and congratulated me for an effort well-done.

Another filled in exactly where the first voice left off. It was simple, direct, and to the point:

"Yes, you've done it, but you now have more than 3,000 miles ahead—some of the world's most dangerous water and weather awaits."

CHAPTER 14

≈≈≈•≈≈≈

ON TO ALASKA—WHERE POLAR BEARS ARE RESTLESS

Two thousand miles to the northwest, deep within the shallow, East Siberian Sea, one of the most storm-tossed and violent areas on the northern Russian coast, two small depressions were forming.

During summer months, low-pressure systems such as these were for the most part benign. But add winter to the mix, and these small seasonal storms would build into ship-killing tempests. While winter had yet to descend on the area, summer was clearly over, and as these depressions grew in strength, they began their eastward tracking towards *Bagan* as we slowly worked our way west.

Low-pressure weather systems are not unusual in that area of the Arctic Sea but their simultaneous formation indicated that, with the onset of winter, conditions would get decisively worse before they got better. Nothing the fifty-seven–foot trawler and crew couldn't handle, but these storms were to be the first in a successive procession from Siberia that would dramatically intensify in the weeks and months to come. Although we had successfully transited The Passage, we were now running behind schedule if we wanted to avoid the worst of the wintry, storm-tossed seas.

We had just spent what I referred to in my journal as "the best day of the trip"—with seas flat and winds less than ten knots out of the east and at our backs. Since our departure from Cambridge Bay, tensions had taken a step back and fatigue had eased greatly. The crew listened to their iPods, read, and slept as we made our way west for Tuktuyaaqtuuq (Tuk), Canada. No more than a two-day's run, the miles slid past our keel as we made a very steady nine knots for *Bagan*'s next destination. The trip was now stepping into "delivery mode" as we began a 3,000-mile race against the clock.

Our ice delay in The Passage had cost us valuable time. The low-pressure systems would continue with greater frequency and more strength, soon making the Beaufort, Chukchi, and Bering Seas all but impassable. The Gulf of Alaska would simply be too storm-tossed for a boat of our size. Even if we could get to Tuk, then on to Barrow, Nome, and through the Aleutian Islands within the next month, there would be no guarantee we'd be able to finish the trip in a single year.

This was not an option for me.

I didn't know if I'd have the emotional strength, motivation or money to finish in a second season.

This is where I had to start balancing determination against practical safety.

We continued to rack up needed miles to the west while the first of the two low-pressure cells made its presence known. What had been the best day of the trip was slowly starting to change. By 4 p.m., what breeze there was had moved east to west, and by 10 p.m. and in approaching darkness, a large swell from the west found us gently rising up its front and gliding down the back, announcing that west had met east and our perfect day had changed for the worse.

By midnight, the day's light and variable winds had increased to 30 knots. *Bagan* was no longer gliding but violently slamming off the crests of this new sharpened wave train from Siberia. The beginning of the final third of the trip, a section that held potential to be the roughest and physically the most demanding, had started in earnest. There was no sleeping below.

Anything that wasn't tied down was being tossed about or launched. With each lurch, staying put on your mattress was impossible. As I lay in my bunk, I designed the perfect solution: a mattress covered in the "male" side of Velcro and a body suit made of the "female" side. Staying in bed was simple, though I'm still working on how to reverse the process to get out of bed.

Velcro suit notwithstanding, I rolled onto watch at 2 a.m. and found Greg with a white-knuckle grip on the wheel. Waves were still breaking against our bow occasionally flooding the foredeck with white water, pin points of phosphorus glowing in the dark, frigid Arctic night. Earlier we'd altered course to the south to try and get closer to shore and perhaps get ourselves more in the lee from the blowing west wind. *Bagan* and her autopilots were doing a wonderful job, but the conditions, large seas, fog, darkness, and potential ice had gotten the best of Greg. I suggested relying fully on the autopilots, but he smiled and kept his eye on the radars, looking ahead for large waves. Although Greg's grip on the wheel had no effect on the steering of *Bagan*, it did give him a small measure of security and confidence.

Earlier that day, when life was a bit more controlled and I was glowing with the success of leaving The Passage, I called Dan and Marcia Streech in Dana Point, California. Dan, president of the company that builds Nordhavn yachts, had cheered me on since the very conception of the trip. Despite our problems with financing, Dan and his wife Marcia remained my dearest and closest friends and they were atop the list of those I wanted to call to report the success of the transit.

The expected scratchy and broken satellite connection did nothing to lessen the impact of the call as Dan and I were speechless, Marcia was in tears of joy. The support and compassion these two friends extended during our call was most definitely one of the three of four events that helped me survive the rest of the trip.

During the call, Dan committed $10,000 to the expedition, a sum we desperately needed and an offer that lifted no small amount of burden from my shoulders.

This wonderfully supportive conversation also helped bring me back to a peaceful reality. Dan reported that the trip had caused a firestorm on the Internet and some armchair sailors had criticized our venture on blogs or other maritime sites, writing that what we were doing was not only irresponsible and reckless but foolish for exposing the crew to such danger. They went on to write that most assuredly were I to get into trouble, I would be the type to send for help immediately and demand that someone bail me out. Later that day, I read those myriad blogs and came away incredibly saddened and hurt.

If these naysayers had taken only a minute to cheer us on, it would have made a world of difference to not only me but to the rest of the crew, their families, and friends as well. To this day, I am shocked how they could deem our efforts irresponsible having never once talked with me or asked a single question.

The latest weather chart showed that the low-pressure system was now settled above us and would be parked there for the next day or so. Behind it another and stronger system was poised to roll in and replace it, assuring that what we were now dealing with was going to worsen. Clinton and Dominique pored over the nautical charts hoping to find a small indent, a barren cove, even a tiny island to hide behind for the next day and a half.

Deciding that being pushed around and rocked about on a 175-pound anchor was better than launching into and off the back of waves with a thirty-knot breeze against us, we got as close to the shore of The Dolphin and Union Straits as possible and tried to get some rest, a move that looked good on paper but left much to be desired.

That afternoon's weather chart download showed us that perhaps 500 miles away, a potentially dangerous second system had stalled and a small window of acceptable weather had opened. If we were lucky, we could take advantage of it and scoot into Tuk, perhaps a day away.

In poor conditions, a boat will always be able to take more than her crew. Inside unsecured books, cans, and loose parts will careen about and make a distracting and frightening racket.

If you hunt down the source of all the noises, lay the offending items on their sides, wedge them into place with a paper towel, dish rag or boxer shorts, all will settle down and suddenly seem manageable. Dominique has mastered this art form, so that while outside the elements seemed to conspire against us with now six- to eight-foot waves and winds peaking at forty knots, life aboard was essentially safe.

"We're sustaining twenty-five knots and at that rate it's going to mean big problems. May hit thirty tomorrow, really dangerous." I didn't know if Clinton was trying to taunt Greg and Chauncey with these exaggerated scenarios or if he was trying to release some of his insecurities. Neither was acceptable and I told them twenty-five knots was merely a bumpy day on Narragansett Bay, and that while what we were now in wasn't comfortable, it wasn't dangerous. When Clinton and I had the pilothouse alone, he grinned and said, "Just trying to scare the greenhorns." A few seconds of silence lay between us, a brief spell of eye contact.

On very rare occasions, if you're very lucky, you get a chance to a look into someone's heart and character—a few brief seconds can provide more than a two-hour conversation. In our two seconds of silence, I knew that Clinton's pronouncements to Greg and Chauncey was as much his trying to "scare the greenhorns" as it was a release of his own lack of confidence.

The events of the past seventy days came rushing up at me, replaying in my mind, and suddenly I saw that with this latest attitude, Clinton was simply not the man, the professional I thought he was. He's a competent sailor, a great mechanic, and can read weather and the water with uncanny skill. But he was far from the man I thought I hired. In that moment of his trying to instill fear into the hearts of two of our less-experienced crewmembers, I'd lost complete faith in Clinton.

We pushed through the continued nasty weather and on August 30 arrived in Tuk for a much-needed break in this small Inuit community of approximately 950 people set in Kugmallit Bay on the south shore of the Arctic Sea. Here we took on what fresh food we could, walked the area, and downloaded weather and ice charts. We had one more potential pocket of ice to deal with and needed to keep an eye on developing low-pressure systems being born farther west in Siberia.

Tuk offered up many examples of how a small community dealt with living above the permafrost. Everything, including a graveyard, was built above ground with the hope that man will recognize and take to heart the changing climate conditions—a situation far beyond the scope of my aim for the trip but one that couldn't be ignored.

In Tuk, I began receiving a flood of congratulatory emails from around the world, cheering us on, sharing and joining in the accomplishment of a successful exit from The Passage. Hundreds of emails filled my inbox from people who had been following every leg of the trip, every blog post. I read each message aloud and shared in the glorious support we were receiving. There was no bigger thrill than to read notes which began, "Hi Sprague and Crew – You don't know me but I've been following your trip..." I did my best to answer each one and found that every time I hit the "send" button, it lifted my spirits and hopes immensely.

Such was the flurry that I contacted my PR and web guy Matt Dutra and asked him to check the recent hits on our website. When we left Newport, we'd had perhaps 300 hits. In the past few weeks, we had amassed more than 27,000.

On September 2, we left Tuk at 6:00 a.m. to start our next leg to Barrow, Alaska, where we had arranged to pick up the hydraulic pump, which, through the help of Marcia Streech's son, Rod Williams, would be waiting for us. We were approximately 500 miles east of Barrow. I had just gotten off watch and was taking refuge in my sleeping bag when Chauncey came into my cabin. Straight to the point he said, "Ice ahead." He face was drawn and gray. My stomach lurched and muscles tightened. No sooner had Chauncey left my cabin that I heard the dreaded throttling back of the engine and felt us slow to a crawl. The inner voices and fears that had plagued me from our previous time in the ice were back with a vengeance and it took everything I had to climb out of that bunk and go up to the pilothouse.

Dominique and Sefton were in the helm seats while Chauncey and Greg stood behind them, all of them staring straight ahead. For 500 yards ahead of us and as far as you could see to the south, running up and out of sight to the north, was once again, an impenetrable sheet of ice.

That area where the Amundsen Gulf blends into the Beaufort Sea is topped by an ever-present massive ice sheet which, seemingly with no reason, moves north and south, all but closing down and then opening up, a passage from Tuk to Barrow.

During the summer months, there's usually always plenty of room, south of the ice sheet perhaps up to 100 miles. From time to time, it will extend south, posing a hazard to anyone trying to cross. What we now saw in front of us was a reminder that not only could it get a bit farther south, but we were about as significant as a piece of floating wood.

The ice charts gave absolutely no indication as to whether this was part of the overall sheet itself or scattered, smaller sheets that could be easily maneuvered. We all stared ahead working with the two radars and trying to see into the quickly falling darkness what we could expect to encounter.

Silence filled the pilothouse. "Shit," I said. "We're fucked," added Chauncey. Sefton sealed the deal with "This is so not good."

By now it was totally dark and although the winds had abated somewhat, we were approaching the ice in darkness with little more than hope and that familiar stomach-churning fear. Sefton and Chauncey took to the foredeck with searchlights. I was at the helm. Dominique was next to me, and Greg was in position on the side decks. We were all once again in a place and situation that none of us had any need to ever find ourselves in again.

The hopes and confidence we'd all felt earlier now seemed to all tumble in around us. It felt as though we had let our guard down, released our vigilance, perhaps allowed ourselves to get a bit cocky and even dared relax and look ahead. Nature had sucker-punched us, decimated our collective reserves of strength. We slowly worked our way toward and into the ice sheet without the group spirit and the silent but determined optimism we had before. We had nothing left. If we were honest with ourselves, and most all of us were, we felt beaten, and all we could do was react with no plan of anything more than one foot at a time.

Chauncey came back into the pilothouse, shaken, exhausted. With complete and drained indifference he said, "It's going to happen again." My response was weak and fake, but I said that this ice was entirely different, that it was only a leading edge and that I'd bet the money in my pocket (none) that we'd be out in a few hours. I based this hollow optimism on absolutely nothing and was hard-pressed to believe it myself. Perhaps I needed to hear some words of encouragement, regardless how shallow, and took comfort in saying them. Whistling past the graveyard.

Again, the gnawing feeling of leading my children to their death came to life. Chauncey left the pilothouse unimpressed, and I sat alone, once again in the deep darkness of soul that I thought I'd left back in Peel Sound. Once again, sheer desperation, loneliness, and fear started to rattle around inside of me.

While I still believed that *Bagan* and crew could continue day after day, mile after mile and arrive in Seattle as hoped, I also felt with tremendous clarity that the trip's success was no longer under consideration. It was black and white, we'd make it or we wouldn't, we'd sink or survive. Gone was the clutter of "what ifs" and "fingers crossed." There was no gray area.

Today we're fine. Tomorrow we could be dead.

No emotion guided this feeling. No reasoning or logic. I had fallen into that state of mental exhaustion where options were a luxury for someone else, and that failure, death, sinking, or drowning was as present and viable as life and success. This new area didn't alter my mood as much as it instilled a philosophy of being reactive instead of proactive. If we got stuck in the ice, we would sink. If we didn't, we'd gain another day. If the storms were early and overpowered us, such was life. I quietly studied the faces and listened to what was being said around me. We were all in the same place: mentally exhausted to the point that would soon test each one of us in potentially deadly terms.

We managed to slide through the sheet for most of the night and by sunrise we were free for what I hoped was the final time. The temperament and properties of this seemingly random ice sheet again drove home the point to all of us that no matter the planning, clever thinking, or electronic advantage, challenging Mother Nature and her powers is a losing proposition.

Witnessing the killing powers behind these ice sheets makes you feel it's personal, that it was in control of your fate, callously marching with malicious intent.

But this very long and dicey night ended with one of the most beautiful and encouraging sights I had ever seen. As the red sun came up the next morning and spread its path of illumination and warmth over the Amundsen Gulf, we all saw a sight that none of us were prepared for—Alaska's North Slope, in particular The Brooke's Range.

This remarkable range of 9,000-foot mountains stretches east to west across Canada's Yukon Territory and well into Alaska. The rising sun had started to spill light across the massive faces of these towering snow-capped mountains, letting us know we were about to take yet another small but remarkably meaningful step.

After almost three months of non-stop traveling, we were soon to be back in the United States, a stunning boost to our collective confidence and determination.

All day we looked south onto these welcoming peaks and although we knew that there was still much awaiting us, we had come a tiny bit closer to achieving our goal.

And then the weather rolled in—again.

With almost perfect timing, another low had gathered strength and seeing the wind move instantly from light and variable to twenty-five knots, sparking steep and sharp waves with a slow clocking of the building breeze.

All that night and into the next morning, we slammed off of what felt like hollow backed waves and were tossed about in no regular fashion. Eating was catch-as-catch-can and sleeping was near impossible. We rotated in and out of watch with very little to say to one another, all keeping an eye on the charts and our steady progress to Barrow, where rest and hopefully the hydraulic pump were waiting. Getting into Barrow was yet another thing.

At 11 a.m., we made the turn to the south into the outskirts of Barrow. Due to the building weather and promise of yet more depressions to come, we anchored in a wide, flat, and very shallow lagoon to the north of town, which at its entrance had a ten-foot bar that required more surfing than actual powering. Six- to eight-foot waves ran past us as we entered the lagoon and exited the storm just outside of it in the Chukchi Sea. All sixty tons of *Bagan* would be lifted and then thrown forward at a healthy nine to eleven knots, like a Laguna Beach surfer. Seeking out an anchorage far enough inside to protect us from the relenting wind, we gently ran aground twice as we made our way through a maze of shallow soundings and muddy reefs. The bottom of the lagoon was made of silt and soft earth, so if we found water too shallow, we simply came to a slow and gentle halt and with a bit of excessive power, backed off and tried another direction.

No sooner was the anchor down then we were hailed by a fishing boat on the VHF radio, welcomed to the anchorage, and warned about "Chewie," a large male polar bear who loved inflatable dinghies. (Two mornings later, we found Big Black to be fairly deflated with two evenly spaced holes in one of her pontoons.)

Barrow and her approximately 5,000-person population proved a valuable stop in many ways. Clinton hunted down and found Judge Karen Hegyi, who had been wonderful in offering to have the needed pump from Niad shipped directly to her address.

He got a ride into town, gathered up the package, had his picture taken with Karen, and extended immense thanks by means of an invitation to *Bagan* for a tour and dinner. The continuous storms rolling down from Siberia had at one point washed out the road from town to our anchorage so, unfortunately, we never were able to see Karen aboard.

We had a few days to kill as for each low pressure cell that held us in place, two more were forming about 1,000 miles to the northwest. Concerned that an early winter was imminent, we became concerned about getting down to Nome. But being held there gave us plenty of chances for filming and still photography of some of the more remarkably disturbing sights we encountered during the five months we would be aboard. Slightly to the north of our anchorage, on a barren and brutally windswept beach, also the farthest northern point in the continental United States, we came across an area which I simply referred to as The Killing Fields.

From August 15 through October 31, Alaskan Inuit engage in what's referred to as "subsistence whaling" here. In fact, when we were about thirty miles north of Barrow, we were warned out of the area over the radio. It seems there was a possibility of our interfering with the hunting of the bowhead whales—that our engine noise would scare off whales. The hunting of the whales is a culturally honored event, we were reminded when we got out to Point Barrow. We had been told that the Point was a whale burial ground, where the whales, once killed, are brought ashore with small boats, cut up, and dispersed. I didn't know what to expect until I got there and was stopped in my tracks by what I saw. The area was strewn with bones in every shape and form. Not the antiseptic, bleached-out bones that I semi-expected, but freshly stripped carcasses. It was not a pleasant sight or smell. The bones, many still with sinew and fat on them, were dark with decay.

All around me was the litter of rot, tangible examples of a cultural act that has been time-honored and rightly respected for years. From my vantage point, it was not a pretty sight but from the view of a person whose ancestors have been hunting and feeding themselves in this manner for generations, this was a way of life that should not know judgment.

With the meat removed, some of the remains are put to hundreds of uses: whalebone sod houses, whalebone art, baleen baskets, even a baleen palm tree. We filmed for as long as we could, the carcasses offering realistic yet abstract views as the rotting flesh and bones were buffeted and pushed about by the continuous gales. From time to time, we'd look out to the ocean, where the Chukchi turned into the Bering, and stared with diminishing hopes at eight- to ten-foot seas pounding ashore, shaking the beach as they beat against the barren sand.

We were going to have to face the weather sooner or later and it was my fervent hope that the evening's weather charts would allow it to be sooner.

I was confident we could make it through, but I had concerns that with an already spent crew, something disturbing and reprehensible lay in front of us.

CHAPTER 15

A FORCED DECISION

"I'm tired of hearing my sister referred to as a bitch!"

Chauncey voiced his concerns loud enough for everyone to hear. Below in my cabin, against the noise of a continuously pounding diesel, his announcement wasn't lost on me. I hadn't been doing much sleeping on a fifty-seven–foot boat with five people, several hundred miles above the Arctic Circle, and two days out of Barrow, Alaska.

We had all exceeded our limits.

Since we left Tuk early on September 7, we had been playing cat and mouse with a series of small but persistent depressions that rolled over us from the northwest. Exhaustion was the norm, far from how we felt when we left Newport. What I'd just heard told me that we'd dipped below this level and if we were going to somehow manage to rise above it again, it would have to be addressed. Getting close to shore and being partially in the lee of the stiff breeze, we dropped the hook by Kukpowruk Pass, even with our "flopper stopper" (two large stainless steel plates "boomed" out over either side of the boat to help damper the rolling while at anchor) rig deployed, *Bagan* was still tossed about like a rag doll and there was little sleep to be found.

We hoped to enter into a small, vaguely charted lagoon we had seen two miles north of us. The charts showed only a small indentation with a color blue that indicated water deep enough for *Bagan* to enter without running aground. We made two attempts but failed. Breaking six-foot waves indicated a bar at the lagoon. Depth gauges all warned us that we were getting into very thin water. All it would take would be to have *Bagan* lifted by one of the combers and slammed into the bottom and the chances of us limping out were pretty slim. With that relentless wave train, if *Bagan* were to be jammed sideways in the uncharted opening, we'd be rolled or swamped in an instant.

Clinton made two nerve-wracking passes that showed no hope of a safe and controlled entrance. He and I said it at the same time, "Let's get outta here," and with that spun *Bagan* on her centerline and steamed back to where we'd anchored earlier that day.

For the next four hours, *Bagan* was tossed about on her anchor, the forty-knot winds catching her, "sailing" her about the massive plough anchor set deeply into the bottom. Those who felt that they could sleep, tried, others simply lay in their sleeping bags in the salon, looking out the ports with hopes of seeing a break in the weather or otherwise lost in deep and far away thoughts. Life aboard had become stuffy, almost intolerant and even Dominique's wonderful cooking had long since left the realm of comforting.

At one point, I awoke from a fitful sleep and I remember thinking I couldn't handle the "cooking" smell anymore. By this point in the trip, more than three months of dwindling optimism and growing dark concerns, everything was setting me on edge.

I tried with all I had to greet each person every "morning" with something resembling a smile but knew all too well that more times than not my hoped-for smile and positive comment fell short. Almost overnight the situation with the winter low pressures, the depressions and storms, had gone from "if and when" to "here and now." The most dangerous third of the trip was now upon us with a vengeance.

That afternoon's weather chart showed the tiniest of windows forming, and a wind dropping in intensity for a few hours before it shifted to the northeast, a direction that, while favorable, would bring stronger gusts. We opted to up-anchor and once again hit the road, before it hit us.

We all rolled in and out of our watches for the afternoon and evening and what sun we were hoping to see was blocked out by quickly traveling, scudding, dark, moisture-laden clouds. The heavy feeling of isolation and oppression that we'd felt for the past few months seemed to be lifting, but only if you stared at it very hard and willed it so.

For the rest of that afternoon and into the night, we ran with eight- to ten-foot seas charging at us from behind, rolling down out of the north, picking *Bagan* up and violently sliding her sideways. So much so that occasionally she'd end up just about on her beam ends and take what seemed like the better part of five seconds to right herself, only to be punched back down onto her port side again. It was building into a white-knuckle storm, but the white wasn't from fear but aggressively trying to hold on.

During my midnight watch, I began to hear a noise that, if I were correct, meant nothing short of disaster for us. From the general area of the starboard stabilizer, I thought I heard the faintest of high-pitch moaning, a quiet but definite long-drawn-out squeal. I tried to sit in denial as long as I could but knew that as soon as I got off watch, I needed to head down to the engine room and take a look at the actual stabilizer arm and external stabilizer, which were working so hard to keep us level during the cold, Arctic pounding we were taking.

While in Barrow, Clinton had replaced the hydraulic pump so I knew it wasn't that but a new problem. Minutes later, I found myself in the engine room staring into the stabilizer locker in disbelief. The arm that connected the actual outside stabilizer wing to the gyro inside was flopping about in its sleeve, creating a larger opening for itself. Imagine your balled right fist wrapped in your left hand. It's a nice tight fit because the left hand can contain all the movement of the fist. Now loosen your left hand by two inches and your right fist will flop around uncontrolled, creating a larger and larger "pocket" out of your left hand. That's the situation I was now looking at. At one point, Chauncey came down to the engine room and joined me, trying to not necessarily assess the current situation but project ahead to the worst scenario.

I couldn't see straight and needed sleep badly. I decided that the next morning I would email Dan Streech at Nordhavn and pick his brain as to what the outcome could be, the worst being that we could lose the external stabilizer wing and breech the hull. Though unlikely, in this neck of the woods it was an answer I needed.

With yet another concern to sing me to sleep, or a vague facsimile of sleep, I awoke at 2 a.m. More to the point, something awoke me. I felt as though something was very wrong and I was all but pulled out of bed because of it. It could very well have been the remnants of a dream, but so strong was the feeling, that I went up to the pilothouse to check in. I walked into a wall of tension and rage. All were up, yet no one was saying anything, more important, no one was answering my questions.

"What's up?"

Silence.

I looked at the instrument and gauges, they showed forty knots, that we were tracking along more or less in the right direction, and the engine temperatures all seemed fine. *Bagan* rolled violently onto her port side.

Dominique was in the helm seat on watch.

"Dom . . . what's going on?" Silence. I noticed that Clinton was in the salon aggressively digging through a drawer of supplies.

I waited a bit longer then asked once more. "If something's going on, I need to know about it and now."

Dominique, in her usual diplomatic and understated way, simply answered back, "All's okay . . . now," and left it at that.

Something had happened and seeing what I saw, feeling what I felt, I was in no mood to try to play understanding trip leader and roll with it as I tried to in the past.

"Dominique, as trip leader, employer, boat owner, and parent, I need to know, now, if there's an issue relating to the safety of the boat or crew."

Dominique's answer was direct and to the point, "Just a bit too much testosterone in the air tonight. All's well now." This woman is going to be an amazing parent or trip leader herself. In those few words, she summed up an unacceptable incident that I was to learn about the next morning. The incident was a part of everyday life when locked aboard a fifty-seven-foot trawler for months at a time with five other people. If it were to happen in the outside world, it would not have been tolerated for a minute.

It seems that when Chauncey was on watch, he'd heard a racket from the computer closet just below the "dashboard" in the pilothouse. He found that the computer tower wasn't lashed down and set permanently in place. Now that *Bagan* was in a washtub being tossed about from rail-to-rail, stem-to-stern, the tower was free to flop and bang up against the bulkhead. Chauncey was extremely concerned about how much the computer could take and dove into the locker to try to secure it. If we lost this computer, we would be left with just our laptop, which had only the navigation program and the basic charts on it. It wouldn't have been the end of the trip, but having to rely on paper charts would have made a very exhausting and demanding trip even more so.

While Chauncey was in the locker trying to wedge the tower in, perhaps get some bungee cords wrapped around it, Clinton came into the pilothouse and immediately said, "What the fuck are you doing? Get your ass out of there!" One thing led to another, accusations and incriminations flew, and the incident was ended with Clinton suggesting to Chauncey, "I ought to kick your ass and now!"

Chauncey didn't shirk from the suggestion.

By first light, the computer was secured, I was back on watch again, the winds were slowly abating, and I found a chance to talk privately talk to both guys, offering them a chance to air feelings rather than continue the conflict. One accepted the invitation, the other brushed it off. I was now officially running the world's most expensive day-care center.

On September 10, about five that afternoon, we had tied up to the steel bulkhead in Nome's inner harbor, and, with engines shut down, we all felt a great and powerful relief that we had managed to check off one more leg. During the previous day's run, we had entered into the Bering Straits and passed Big and Little Diomede Island, half-U.S. (east of the International Dateline), half-Russian (west of the International Dateline) and two-and-a-half miles apart. I had spoken with Dan Streech earlier and he greatly put my mind at ease about our stabilizer situation. While he said he could try to get a new sleeve to us, we shouldn't be concerned about future damage because however ugly it looked and sounded, the arm could (and did) work very well and would never truly break or snap.

Securely tied to the steel bulkhead in Nome's inner harbor, the first thing we arranged was to take on 1,200 gallons of diesel and take Dominique out to as good of a dinner as we could find. Our legs not quite being what they had been even a few weeks ago, we got about as far as a pizza restaurant and fell face-first into our pies. Very little was said at dinner, as the energy to start and maintain a conversation about anything was long since gone.

Later the next day, as Chauncey, Sefton, Greg, and I were poking about town, Greg opened a subject that would greatly change the scope of the trip. "Someone better talk with Clinton about his hours."

My heart sunk. I was sick to death of hearing about potential problems or comments about things detrimental to the trip. "Tell me," was about all I could come back with. Greg reported that after the previous night's wonderful dinner, Clinton went out for a few beers and stumbled back aboard at 6:30 in the morning, seemingly feeling no pain. Nothing I wanted or needed to hear. I looked at Chauncey and Sefton, with small nods they backed up Greg's concern. I'd had enough and returned to *Bagan* to deal with a situation I did not want to escalate.

Walking back to *Bagan* I felt physically sick. Again I had to fight to keep this latest news from stripping every remaining ounce of pride and belief in the rest of the trip out of me. The inner, dark voices were telling me that I was completely fed up with the behaviors, the building problems, and the over-whelming feeling of lack of accomplishment. I was in tremendous and total financial debt for absolutely nothing other than pushing a wonderful boat and crew to their limits. I could no longer rise to the occasion; inside I caved. I hated the trip with everything I had, which by this point was next to noth-ing, wished to God I'd never gone to that long-ago dinner in New York when I was asked about my "ultimate" adventure.

When I got back aboard, I could smell what seemed to me the stale, sickly stench of cheap booze. Up on the boat deck I found a pile of wet and muddy clothes, reeking of diesel, tucked, hidden, under Big Black. Dominique was at her computer, catching up on email. I asked her where Clinton was. Without looking up she simply said, "Still in bed."

I planted myself in the helm seat in the pilothouse and waited. I wasn't mad, I wasn't fuming, I wasn't ruminating about what I should say, I was simply worn out.

About 2:30 that afternoon, Clinton entered the pilothouse, asked what was happening, and gave a big smile. I had nothing to return. All I could manage was "What you do on your time is your business, but this shit's stop-ping now." He smiled and went down to the salon to hear Dominique's more vocal appraisal.

Up to that point in the trip, I had tried to give everyone the benefit of the doubt, tried to honor and roll with each request, did what I thought would be for the best of the boat and crew, and extended into areas I didn't have to. I'd paid both Clinton and Dominique up front for not only the prep time for the trip but for a projected six months the actual trip was to take. I paid all transportation and food for all the crew and always paid for rental cars and extras. I'd done my best to see that no one was without more than a trip of this nature would demand. I say this not to try to portray a sense of selflessness but to try to indicate my belief in the project as well as my crew. The fact that on multiple occasions I had to deal with Clinton and what were reported by others to be his onshore antics was extremely debilitating. I recognized the man's excellence and entrusted him with not only *Bagan* but also my family and dream. In the course of one long evening out, I felt he had tossed it all back in my face.

I wasn't sure at that moment if he had registered my disapproval, but found I needed to get off the boat. I wanted to walk. I wanted to walk as long and as far as I could and if my walking took me all the way back to Newport, so much the better. I headed out onto a long and straight paved road and put one foot in front of the other as fast as I could. I had never felt as betrayed and alone as I did then.

As my concern grew, I realized I had no one to turn to, no one from whom to seek advice. I had been feeling this sense of isolation for far too long now and it was winning. I needed guidance and motivation and had nowhere to turn. It was only a matter of a few weeks ago when, in the ice, we all felt the complete and abject loss of options—that the ice was going to do with us as it wished. I now felt the very same way, but about the trip and my life as a whole.

I started to walk faster, trying to build up and burn out a good sweat. Shortly into it I dropped to the ground as though I'd stepped on a 220-volt live wire and knew immediately that the toe was back. My toe felt like it was being cut by a white-hot knife and once again there was nothing I could do about it. I'd gone about a mile by this point, which ironically enough had me at the entrance to Nome's airport. And there I sat. I fantasized about getting onto a plane, any plane, taking off for a destination unknown, and doing a fly-by over *Bagan*, dropping my credit cards out the window and wishing them all the very best of luck. On my fantasy plane, I turned to look about at fellow passengers and gladly saw Chauncey, Dominique, Sefton, and Greg all sitting with me. The trip had ended and we were all now going someplace warm and stress-free. A heavy blast of freezing Arctic air brought me back to my senses and reminded me that we had perhaps another 2,500 miles to go, were running against a ticking seasonal clock, had two more months of gales ahead of us, and, in all likelihood, were not going to make it in one season.

Yet as I was heading back to *Bagan,* I had as wild an experience as I'd had the whole trip. Something in the air caught my attention. An aroma came at me and for the life of me, I couldn't identify it. I stopped to try and figure out what this powerful combination of sweet and acrid was when it dawned on me that I smelled the simple scent of shrubbery and damp earth. We'd been above the Arctic Circle for so long that my nose had seemed to have forgotten the scent of vegetation.

Arriving back at *Bagan,* I found that Greg, Chauncey, and Sefton had gone out to pan for gold and do some hiking. I downloaded some email and gladly read some more messages of congratulations plus received second and third demands for payments on bills.

If the Arctic offered anything, it offered a wonderful safety net of "Come and get me."

I answered emails, paid what bills I could, and started thinking about the next leg to Dutch Harbor in the Aleutian Chain. Because of the dramatic change in weather and seasonal patterns, "planning" was limited to that of perhaps a few days, not weeks, out. It was now a given the trip could end any day, for if the lows continued to grow in intensity, we could be locked in until the spring.

I went to bed early but suddenly found myself awake at 2:00 a.m., and while I hoped with every part of my being that it were a only a dream, I'd awoken to shouting, shouting which equally sickened me as much as it terrified me. "Man in the water . . . Man in the water!" It was Chauncey's voice and the rushing of footsteps up to the pilothouse assured me that this was no dream. I was outside as quickly as possible and what I saw was pathetic and infuriating.

Clinton and a friend he'd made in town were standing outside on land, on the opposite side of the steel bulkhead we'd been tied up to for two days. In the thirty-degree water was a third friend who was slowly going into what appeared to be shock. Clinton was soaking wet, shaking uncontrollably, and getting paler by the moment. Amid the confusion, I went to a ladder on the bulkhead and helped fish the remaining friend out of the Arctic water. I wish that I could say that at that moment I saw red, but the situation was so surreal that all we could do was react.

Dominique and Greg started to get a soaking wet Clinton back aboard. He was incapable of doing this himself. All he could do was mutter that he was fine between frozen lips, then laugh. By this point, he was no longer able to stand and kept falling out of their grasp. Chauncey and Sefton had earlier heard a splash, and rushing quickly outside, they found Clinton in the water between boat and bulkhead and trying to get himself out over *Bagan*'s stern. Then they heard another splash and found one of his new friends struggling in the water as well. By this point, the rest of us were all up and out of bed trying to contain the situation.

As Greg and Chauncey tried to get Clinton inside, he fell yet again on the boat, nearly knocking his head against a steel cleat and laughing all the while. As far as I was concerned, that was it. I had neither time nor energy left for drama and babysitting. I told Clinton clearly that he was off the project, that I'd had enough.

I told him that he had until noon the following day and with that Greg got him down below into a warm shower and into bed. As he passed me on his way below, he stopped. We locked eyes and determinedly held each other's gaze. I had no feeling. My concern at that point was only for the kids and *Bagan*. Perhaps thirty seconds later, Clinton looked down at the floor. I asked Greg to get him below and out of my sight.

Sefton, Chauncey, Dominique, and I stood quietly in the pilothouse, no one saying a thing, all eyes elsewhere.

Finally Chauncey broke the silence with, "Jesus, that was intense," and walked down to the salon; slowly, the others joined him.

The five of us held a 3 a.m. meeting so that all the blanks could be filled in for me and I could give each a chance to air their feelings. We were united in what we felt we had to do but against my better judgment, I felt that in the morning we should have one more meeting, including Clinton, and see if there was even an ounce of contrition. Otherwise we would leave him on shore, try to grab the weather window, and leave that afternoon.

None of us slept. It was 10 a.m. and Dominique had twice been below to notify Clinton that we were all meeting, but each time he laughed at her request and went back to sleep. I then went down at 10:30 and told him the same. I let him know that we were all having a meeting, him included, about his future on the boat and that we couldn't begin without him.

"Yes sir, be right there," he said. But he returned to sleep. Fifteen minutes later I went back down and told him again.

"I don't care," he replied.

Fifteen minutes after that I went down for one final time, told him that his absence spoke for him, and he had two hours to be off the boat. He once more returned to sleep.

An hour passed and there'd been no movement from below. I went down to Clinton's cabin again, by this time enraged at what seemed to me his total lack of respect for *Bagan* and the crew.

Trying not to vent my rage, I opened the door to Clinton's cabin, found him still asleep, and told him he had fifteen minutes. He bolted upright and said, "Jesus, give me more time than that," seemingly unaware of our previous warnings.

At 2 p.m. we shook hands all around, I told him that from the bottom of my heart I wished him only the best, he and Dominique shared some words on the foredeck (with Greg, Chauncey, Sefton, and I strategically placed around the boat, were these words to be anything but remorse and well-deserved guilt) and with that, Clinton Bolton was off the boat.

Clinton had helped so much to get *Bagan* prepared, but as I saw him walking away with his possessions in black garbage bags, I felt he had somehow let us down. He had been paid up front for his efforts yet wasn't finishing the trip. His parting words were biting: "I'm outta this shithole boys; I have two months of paid vacation waiting for me."

We were aiming for a 4 p.m. departure from Nome and, as usual, many things had to be done before our departure, especially this departure. Before leaving Newport, someone asked me what I felt to be the most dangerous part of the trip, the icebergs or The Passage itself.

I remember answering saying that what concerned me the most was the Bering Sea. It is shallow with a fairly good north-setting current. The lows pour out of the north and the combination of all three makes for something that was already keeping me up at nights. We were hours away from this sea and I found that once again the stakes increased. None of this was lost on any of the crew. The potential for things far worse than what we'd experienced to date could happen and each one of us was focused, alert but exhausted. A healthy and honest fear was in the boat, a fear that we all admitted to readily, a far healthier response than the one that we just witnessed.

As the days were to roll by, I tried not to but am sure that I did preach to Sefton, Chauncey, and Dominique. That admitting fear and fault was about as noble a thing that one could do for themselves and that admission of shortcomings something which was to be welcomed and not run from. I've no idea if these thoughts were met with complete understanding or loving patience, but I know that I felt better for saying them. The lesson was fresh and far from theoretical.

Before we left Nome, I had assigned Greg to the engine room and told Sefton that he would be running the foredeck as usual but that he was now in charge of downloading the weather charts twice a day. We were now a man down and, while we all had our plates full, I needed to divide up the new responsibilities the best that I could without overwhelming anyone.

After his first thirty minutes in the engine room, Greg had come back with a report about the state of the engine, wing engine and generator as well as reserves of fluids and filters—a report I found to be unfortunately far different than what I'd been previously led to believe the state of things were. Sefton had downloaded the latest charts and projected our conditions for the next three days out.

It was here that something new and disturbing came up inside of me that I could no longer ignore. Deep inside there lurked a concern about my handling of the next few legs. While trapped in the ice, I had seen in my mind's eye a thin but solid black line, just off to the side, in my peripheral vision. When I looked directly at it, it would vanish. Yet when I looked ahead, I could see this line slowly move in and then move away again. It wasn't close nor did it present any danger, but due to the mere fact that it existed at all told me that it was a line not to be toyed with, a line which I should strongly honor, a line not to get too close to for if you did, and it suddenly chose to move in closer, and I were to find that I'd accidentally crossed it, there'd be no coming back to this side and all sense of reality and purpose would be dramatically redefined.

This line was to be in my frame of reference for the rest of the trip and as we headed out into the Bering Sea it moved in closer and would stay there, taunting and teasing, daring me to approach and cross it as we powered toward the unknown horrors ahead.

CHAPTER 16

A PARENT TAKES OVER

It was now a race.

We had a three-day weather window to allow us to get into and navigate the 650-mile Bering Sea, one of the world's most dangerous and unpredictable bodies of water. With an average depth of 150 feet, even small storms would whip up lethal waves.

I had been concerned about the Bering Sea since we left Newport and now that we were in it, I wanted to waste no time getting through and out.

We'd found a shortcut through the Aleutians farther east, so we scrapped the idea of going to Dutch Harbor and tried to gain time by heading straight for Unimak Pass, about 200 miles up the chain.

We were just over 100 miles out of Nome when I heard laughter. The tension undermining the experience for the past 5,000 miles was gone. For the first time since I can remember in the trip, there was palpable joy. The stress and complications were still present but one concern had been taken off the table—we were no longer walking on eggshells. During a watch change between Greg and me, from the depths of the engine room the same screeching sound we'd heard so many times earlier on the trip started again. With the toughest leg of the trip still facing us, we would need our stabilizers desperately. We couldn't afford a hydraulic breakdown at this point, especially from a new pump. In a flash, Greg was off and into the engine room. I watched him on the remote cameras as he studied the problem for a bit then dove in with wrenches. Thirty minutes later, the screeching had stopped and Greg was back. "I just adjusted the mounting bracket, no magic." I wondered if it had ever been installed properly. The first pump was new when we'd left Newport and guaranteed for thousands of hours. We were now on our third pump inside of four months. Thankfully, we didn't hear a peep from it for the rest of the trip.

Early in the morning of the second day, Sefton downloaded weather charts again and assured me the systems were holding and if we were going to get any real breeze, it would be just as we were going through the chain the next evening. Chauncey was busy filming and cleaning up on deck. Dominique was starting dinner and the mood was tension-free. We saw humpbacks in the distance and tried to work our way over to them for filming. We couldn't, but even this small frustration was met with gales of laughter.

I felt as though I was living amid a miracle. Here were my kids, and we had just done what few before us had managed, we had transited the Northwest Passage. We were together, laughing, sharing, and loving one another. Fifteen years ago, I couldn't have even dreamed of such a scenario. Now the family was together and we were united in our goal of getting to Seattle and never drifting apart again.

At one point, Chauncey came into the pilothouse where I'd been writing. He sat next to me and said, "Do you realize what's happening? What's happened? Sprague, this is incredible." He paused then turned to me, "No single other event has ever had such a monumental impact on me as our time together—and in the ice!" We remained silent for a bit, looking at one another. Sefton walked through the area. "Having a good time kiddo?" I asked. He smiled and nodded his head. We were mentally exhausted, all physically beaten up, but as I looked about, listened, and watched, I knew that I was blessed beyond any viable description.

"Guys, once we get through The Bering, *Bagan* will be back in her home waters and I think we'll finally be able to catch our breaths. You're going to love Alaska. It's beautiful. We just need to get through The Bering and we're home free."

On September 15 at 8:30 p.m., *Bagan* powered from the Bering Sea into the Gulf of Alaska and proceeded to get the pounding of her life. Twenty-knot breezes and two-foot seas changed quickly to forty-knot winds and ten-foot seas. The mountainous Aleutians were throwing violent wind gusts down onto us. These heavy and very large pockets of air—williwaws— would roll in from The Bering, crest the tops of the mountains and while gathering deadly speed, roll down the southern faces and slam into us and anything else within a twenty-mile radius.

As dark was falling, we found ourselves trying to get the simplest understanding of these powerful blasts that would, from time to time, exceed fifty knots. In pitch darkness, we headed directly offshore where we found the conditions to be worse because the wave train had had a chance to grow, slamming us onto our side by forces from all directions at once. We'd then turn back toward shore to tuck into the lee of the barren and brutal mountains, to no avail. At one point, I stood in the pilothouse looking at the wind gauge. It was sustained at forty-five knots and was literally blowing around the compass, coming from every point on the dial within a minute. Sefton was beside me and watched. He summed it up best as he said, "This is surreal—never seen anything like this." I agreed and immediately asked him, "Thoughts?" He shook his head and went to make what was going to be the first of many cups of black coffee.

Regardless of the direction we headed *Bagan*, she'd get the tar kicked out of her. One moment we'd be picked up and thrown on her side, the next she'd slam violently off the back of a wave, then she'd surf at a dangerous speed. Slow, fast, it didn't matter. We were locked into the blackest of moonless nights. Greg took the helm for a bit as I suited up and went out on deck to try and get a feel for the wave train. Opening the downwind door, I could feel the air being sucked out of *Bagan* before I hit the freezing air curling around the pilothouse and lashing out at my face. Violent, tortuous winds blew the tops off of waves coming from seemingly every direction. In 40,000 miles of offshore work, including riding out a three-day, seventy-knot gale, I'd seen nothing like this.

Once out of my gear and back into the helm chair, I asked Sefton to get us weather data and Dominique to pull out the Coast Pilot—a book of basic descriptions of the area and its islands for the commercial fleet—and try to find us anything in the way of an anchorage within 50 miles.

Seven hours later, we were snug in Cold Bay, Alaska, tucked up inside the small anchorage and licking our wounds. The city of Cold Bay—with a population of about eighty—is about one-third of the way southwest down the Aleutians, 650 miles from Anchorage.

We'd read that it abounded with caribou, fox, and brown bears and even had two active volcanoes. All of this was lost on us. The past twelve hours left us with only energy to sleep. Our exit from the Bering Sea and our welcome into the Gulf of Alaska was about as rough as it could get, yet we all took comfort in the fact we were now in the Pacific Ocean, a very large step toward the end of the trip.

Noticing that morning that the water tank was nearly empty, I went below to manually run the water maker. Twenty minutes into the procedure, I realized I hadn't made a gallon of fresh water. From time to time, we all get to that place inside where we just can't take any more and walk away, dusting off our hands off saying, "Well, that's that." As much as I wanted it to be now, this wasn't one of those times. We needed water. To get water, we needed a working water maker. I went back up to the pilothouse and searched for previous notes about the conversation held back in St Anthony's with the manufacturer.

There weren't any. This wasn't anything I needed to share with the crew yet, so I headed back down to the engine room determined to find a solution. And in this case, there was one. The manual diversion valve was not engaging, but I coaxed it into place. I wasn't sure how long it would last, but I kept that thought to myself.

As we got back on the road that afternoon, it looked as though we'd stepped back through Alice's "Looking Glass" in the right direction. At some point in the tempest of the previous night, the landscape around us drastically changed, for we were now surrounded by tall, green grasses and muted-brown marshes backed by snow-capped mountains. The wind speed had dropped and we watched as these tall and lush offerings gently waved and bowed in the breeze. The sky had the steep gray pallor of winter, and the air was filled with the threat of snow, but at least what we now looked out into had a semblance of familiarity and we no longer had that spooky "back side of the moon" feeling.

We were a step closer to home but we had a long, long way to go. Winter was in the air and from what Sefton was showing me on the latest weather charts, we should expect more of what we'd just come through.

Our next planned stop was Sitka, where we were going to have to say goodbye to Greg, who needed to get back to his business and family. Two months away had taken a toll on him, and I couldn't ask him for any more of his time. With the expected gales that were going to be rolling in from the north, Sitka wasn't going to be a straight shot. Once again referring to the Coast Pilot, Dominique found us many tucked-away anchorages that we could duck into to wait out the storms. By this point, we were running behind and the odds of us not being able to make it to Seattle were growing by the day, if not by the hour.

That afternoon, we started working our way out of Cold Bay and farther east into the Gulf. We were between systems for a bit and the Gulf that I had promised everyone was in evidence. Humpbacks made appearances while bald eagles fished the waters around us. A blue-sky day spread from horizon to horizon and *Bagan* once again hissed along through the water at eight-plus knots. There wasn't a lot of chatter aboard, just occasional mono-syllabic small talk that had a welcome lightness to it. For the past four days, there hadn't been cross look or word, which helped to prevent any further mental and physical exhaustion. The depths we now found ourselves at would take months to recover from. Friendly smiling eyes were hollow and warm smiles were a flash, both requiring more energy than any one of us had. At this point, it was the concept of family, Greg included, that held us together.

At 6:00 p.m., we tied up to the floating docks of Humboldt Harbor on Popof Island, about 575 miles west of Anchorage. Dark clouds had been building around us and almost to the moment we shut down our engines, winds filed in and the heavens opened. Despite the need for sleep, we all donned foul-weather gear and went ashore. Darkness was falling earlier and between the driving rain and the onset of the dark and damp gloom of night, we were back aboard within hours, sitting in the warm and cozy interior while gales raged outside. In our short walks, we gathered what information we could and met a few fishermen as they came down to lay extra lines on their boats for the upcoming blow. Over beef stew, we compared notes on what we'd learned. Chauncey's news was the most sobering I'd heard since we left Newport: a captain of a larger fishing boat—well into hundreds of feet long—asked where we'd been and where we were thinking of going.

Our news of transiting the Northwest Passage was met with a very neutral gaze but our intentions of getting to Seattle this season raised an eyebrow: "Rule of thumb around here is to be off The Chain by September 12," he said. It was now September 18. He looked at *Bagan* then at his boat. "You're too small. Hell, we're too small for some of this weather."

Again I felt that familiar angst. The questions, the concerns, the fears and the isolation of not being able to turn to someone and ask, "What should we do?" It was far more complicated than a simple question and answer and by now, all that hung in balance began with and ended with the lives of my three children. While I felt fully capable of making rational day-to-day and hour-to-hour decisions, I'd lost touch with the overall picture and sat staring out the port, looking at the rain fly sideways past the boat.

Despite being tucked in among many large and broad-beamed commercial fishing boats, the wind blasted our starboard side and we were pushed up against the old floating wooden dock repeatedly. If it was this rough in the protected marina, what was going on out in the Gulf?

As I crawled into my sleeping bag that night, the wind and rain roared outside. Do we call it quits here? Will the weather abate? Are we indeed too small to be here, and where do I leave *Bagan* for the winter? I needed answers I didn't have. I needed an overview with which I felt I'd lost touch. In the darkness of the gale-driven Alaska night as well as the familiar darkness of my soul, I needed answers and direction.

I needed an angel. And I got one.

We slept soundly that night. As the storms lashed down, rain drumming on the decks above us, no one stirred until after 10:30 the next morning, when I took my first sip of black tea. I wondered who the bearded, dripping wet and smiling man now in front of me in the pilothouse was. He seemed to know me and for the life of me I didn't know him. Yet his smile and warmth were something I'd never soon forget.

It appeared that when Greg awoke far earlier than the rest of us that morning, he went out in the maelstrom to look at the boats, meeting and talking with anyone walking onto or off of their boats, as was his habit. He'd come to the fishing vessel *Shady Lady,* introduced himself to the captain and owner Dan Veerhusen, and extended an invitation to him to come join us board *Bagan.* I think he arrived before Greg.

Every now and again a person walks into your life that holds a key to your future and happiness. And if you're really blessed, this person is also someone you like from the start. Dan was that person. We all took to him immediately and sat in rapt silence as he showed us charts on the best way to transit the Gulf in this weather, find the most secure hiding holes and recognize what to watch for if the weather was going to turn foul. Dan was a tremendously valuable source of information and his generosity and warmth saved us in more ways than we then knew.

We stayed at the docks another day, waiting for a break in the weather and slowly walked our way through the low-lying, windswept town of Sand

Point Alaska. It was a company town in that most front yards held some commercial fishing gear. We later wandered through Trident Seafood, the big employer there, and found our way to the ship's store, which was nothing short of heaven. No fancy sunglasses, no cute t-shirts or flip-flops, simply real gear for real boats in a real ocean—and telephone calling cards which we all bought by the dozen.

Walking back from Trident, I encountered a sight that makes me smile to this day. The rain was coming down sideways and the temperature couldn't have been out of the thirties. Outside of the small breakwater, the seas were piling up against it, occasionally sending plumes of white spray through the cold air. I was buried deep into my gear and thermals when I saw an item that made me feel as though I were on a tropical island.

A tree.

A small and skimpy tree; a Charlie Brown Christmas tree; but a tree.

It was green, had limbs and scrawny roots, maybe even a resident bird or two. It was just about the most beautiful tree I'd ever seen. A picture of that twisted, skinny, and beautiful tree now sits on my desk as I write this.

The next morning, September 19, an hour before first light at 6 a.m., we dropped the lines and headed back out. With Dan's guidance, we now had a strategy to deal with the Gulf until we could work our way down to Sitka, the beginning of Alaska's Inside Passage. Earlier in the morning, I'd listen to a weather forecast from the National Oceanic and Atmospheric Administration (NOAA) on the VHF and had learned that we had a twenty-four–hour window to get as far down the road to the east as we could. The long-range forecast proved to be less than good but with the knowledge of these few anchoring holes where we could hide out, I felt a flicker of cheer and hope.

By noon that day, we were well on our way heading east and in the middle of Shelikof Strait, a passage running from southwest to northeast about forty miles wide and 150 miles long. It separates the mainland of Alaska to the north and Kodiak and Afognak Islands to the south. On the northern end is Prince William Sound, second only to the Bay of Fundy for dangerous currents. It also acts as a funnel for all water and air that moves through, trapped by the towering and rugged Aleutians to the north. For the past hour, we had been hit by forty-knot winds from the northeast with a counter setting current of up to three knots from the west. Once again, we were getting battered and slammed and, while we were making good progress, we were far from comfortable or anything near a cruising speed. By this time, it was impossible to predict where we'd be and when.

Once again, *Bagan* leapt and pounded off the back of waves at times coming to a complete standstill as she ran into the back of the next one. She'd stall out, shudder, and then slowly regain momentum only to climb, slam, and shudder to a stop again. We were aiming for Geographic, a small harbor Dan had told us about, but it was out of reach. Geographic had a straightforward but narrow opening, one that even in the best of conditions I wouldn't like to try at night. None of us had the stamina or determination to attempt a blind entrance. So once again, Dominique sought a suitable stopover venue for that night.

At one point, we had taken a particularly bad hit and *Bagan* simply landed on her side and shook furiously.

As she gained in momentum and speed once again, a call came in over the VHF, "*Bagan... Bagan... Bagan... Western Venture. Over.*" After all the thousands of miles and months away, to hear our name over the airwaves was a complete shock. I sheepishly answered and quickly found that I was talking to the captain of a large commercial fishing vessel to our north who'd been watching our progress, or lack of it. In the short conversation he said that we "looked great!" If he could have only seen it from our side. He told us we "were too small to be on The Chain at this time of year" and that "Captain Dan had put out the word to all in the fleet to keep an eye out for us."

For the next week, we dodged weather systems and hid when we could. The trip was now a day-to-day roll of the dice and any miles we could make were miles closer to Seattle. Like our situation in the ice, we wanted to push on despite the gales until we had no options left. We could either be at the docks in Seattle, in a secluded but secure marina in Alaska, or on the bottom.

Home Cove, Fox Farm Bay, Hinchinbrook, Indian Cove, Sitka. Apart from all of the most basic of entries, the ship's log ends there. Not because of one calamity or event but because down a person we were too beat to fill it out on a regular basis. What sleep we got was never enough, what food we ate produced little to top off our reserves of energy. Each person met his watch in a timely and disciplined manner but that was the limit. I knew that at some point we might need everyone for an all-out effort. With only hours between storms, we'd power until darkness or exhaustion if not both and sit in the current hole, whipped around by gale-force winds, blasted by the combination of sleet and rain, diesel heater all but keeping up with the descending winter. Each day I watched as less and less color came to the faces of the crew, dark circles growing deeper. Reflexes were becoming dulled and laughter was muted. If we had a 6 a.m. departure, I would be up at 5 a.m. listening to various weather bands trying to glean what hopes of optimism I could. More times than not, the computer-generated voice called for "gales" and "full gales expected with six- to eight-foot seas."

In the dark, I'd weigh my options, try to push the numbers as much as my addled dyslexic brain could and, on several occasions, found that I would just lie by omission to my family. "It's not going to be pretty today but nothing we can't handle."

One morning, as we made an early dawn's move through Hinchinbrook Pass, NOAA and my optimism had it entirely wrong, almost deadly wrong. With the unexpected and sudden force of the new gale battering against a countercurrent and shallow shelf, within minutes we found ourselves going up and over twelve- to fifteen-foot seas that had little resemblance to ocean swells. They were sharp and hollow-backed and tossed *Bagan* onto her port side, picked her up then smashed her onto her starboard side. With decks awash, *Bagan* was none too appreciative but didn't miss a beat nor ship a drop of water below. Her occupants came out of the experience with far less equanimity.

On October 1, a gray, cold, and damp day, we entered into the harbor of Sitka in a steady but light drizzle. It had been almost two weeks since we'd last landed at a dock, two weeks of a constant and debilitating pounding. If we weren't pushed by wind and waves, we were in rains that were all but a blackout.

We received our berth assignment from Sitka's Harbor Master and, while turning to line ourselves up for a port landing, alarms engaged. Alarms I'd never heard before. We still had full-engine control but it was obvious that the alarms were connected to the bow thruster, from which I got no response when I activated it.

Despite the alarms and level of exhaustion, we made a perfect landing, just kissing the dock and staying there. Engine off, lines secured, I asked Greg to head down to the engine room and take a quick look to see if there was any obvious indication as to what had caused the alarms. He was back inside of ten minutes telling me we had no hydraulic fluid left. I was somewhat surprised as while in Humboldt Harbor I remember topping the reservoir off. Regardless, it was now empty. "Probably the leak," Greg reassured me, which did anything but. "What leak?" I asked. "Clinton showed me a leak in one of the hoses up by the bow when we were storing gear before we left Newport."

How many more surprises remained, and what potential did they hold to endanger the trip?

After saying our goodbyes to Greg, taking on 1,200 gallons of fuel, buying extra filters, good meals on shore, and trying to catch up on sleep and gain back some energy, we left Sitka and started in on our leg down to Ketchikan.

We all needed a break, a real break not just a rest. We all had been pushed beyond our limits. I strongly felt as though each time I asked the crew to push that little much harder, they did, but each time dipped into shallow reserves that dangerously were never quite replenished. They always answered the need but also always came out of it that much more depleted. Good meals ashore and uninterrupted sleep on a cramped and smelly boat weren't going to do it. Sefton and Chauncey hadn't had a good night's sleep in months because they had taken to sleeping on the settees of the salon. We needed to be off *Bagan* and away for a week. I floated a plan past them that once we reached Ketchikan, we'd leave *Bagan* there for two weeks and each of us would take a week away. I told them I'd buy them each tickets to wherever in the States they wanted to go for their week. I'd deal with the credit card consequences later.

As I'd hoped, this brought relief, motivation, and smiles of joy. Yet the smiles weren't what they'd been when we were in Newport four months ago. There was simply no inner energy left in any of them to completely show their appreciation and delight. Yet some things you don't need words for as just the easing of the concern lines on their faces told me this break was what was needed. It wasn't a truly selfless gesture on my part. I needed to get back to New York and California for some business. More important, I, too, desperately needed a break. By this time, just brushing my teeth required all the energy and optimism I could muster. The final leg from Ketchikan to Seattle was approximately 650 miles and I wanted for us all, as well as *Bagan*, to arrive in the best shape possible—if possible at all.

Little did we know at the time that during this last mini-leg to Seattle, we were to take one more hit, a massive and terrifying hit that was as close to disaster and sinking as we would get during our five-month, 8,500-mile trip, a hit which was seconds away from the possible drowning and death of my family.

CHAPTER 17

STORMY IN SEATTLE

And then there were four.

As I flew back into Ketchikan, the plane was buffeted by blasts of another cold and wind-driven rainy night. In the dark gloom, I walked the half-mile back to the marina where *Bagan* had been resting for the past 10 days. In the time I was gone, it felt as though we had skipped autumn and were now on the edge of a quickly approaching winter. The break had given me—and I hoped the rest of the crew—time to regroup, repower, and summon up the strength for the remaining 650-mile push to Seattle. Dominique had gone back to Newport to see her father and friends. Sefton went to Denver for a slightly belated birthday celebration, and Chauncey flew into southern California to visit friends, bask in the sun, and surf.

As I walked down the docks to the boat, the windy and wet night failed to offer comfort. Nor did it provide motivation and excitement for the next few weeks of travel. A cold rain soaked docks that glistened in the marina's security lighting. Fishing boats tugged and moaned at their lines and the wind-driven rain worked its way down past my upturned collar. Once aboard, we greeted each other but not with the same fervor one would expect when facing the start of what was to be our final leg. It was clear that we were all still tired.

We happily compared notes as to what we did on our breaks, whom we saw, how much sleep we got, and how surreal our past five months seemed. We were flattered and greatly surprised by how many people were following the trip. During my break, in Dana Point, in front of perhaps 250 people attending Nordhavn's boatowner's Western Rendezvous, I gave a talk. While I was happy to present what we had accomplished, I felt odd as I spoke. I knew the trip was far from over and that in a few days I'd be back aboard, facing perhaps one of the potentially worst legs of the trip.

In many ways, the true adventure was about to begin. Winter was quickly approaching, fishing boats were leaving their docks with greater apprehension, and full gales could and would pop up without notice potentially pinning us down for days if not weeks. This final hellish effort was going to be met head-on by four family members who in that past five months and 4,500 miles had grown together as one unlike any family has ever had the opportunity to do.

Our plan was to leave the dock before first light the next day, around 5:30 a.m. We were hoping to run as far as we could and, with the help of a tide, getting perhaps 80 miles to 100 miles farther down the road. Shortly before bed, I had asked Sefton to meet me in the pilothouse. I wanted to present him with something, which for a father at least, was to be the pinnacle of any father-son relationship—something that had me realize what life was all about, an item which would allow me to move into my remaining years knowing that his and my relationship would forever be altered in the most powerful and meaningful of ways.

"Are you kidding? No way..." which was exactly what I expected this now-man standing in front of me to say. "Are you sure??"

Over the journey, I'd been watching as my son had grown from a young man into a resourceful and competent man. He had faced the deadliest of adversities with the greatest of equanimity. When needed, he had provided the most assuring solace that any man twice his age and experience would.

He had faced personal and natural challenges that few, if any, ever see, and each time came through it in a far better standing than I could ever have dreamed of doing at his age. The time had come. As I placed *Bagan*'s keys in Sefton's hand, his beaming smile of self-assured pride betrayed his eyes of a quizzical concern. "She's all yours now. You'll be taking us home. I've been watching you all summer and you're ready."

The question now: Was I?

I had full confidence in his getting us to Seattle but would my heart allow and let go of this once little boy to step into full-fledged manhood? No more poignant moment existed between father and son and as I write this, my eyes flood with the power of the moment of transfer and transition.

As I lay in my bunk later that night, my mind swirled with emotions that ran the gamut of what the next few weeks would mean. And praying that I had the stamina. Although life aboard had calmed considerably, I could still "see" that black line in my mind's eye and I was fearful of crossing it. I was in sensory overload. I tried my best to temper all of these feelings but knew we still had a very long way to go, that the bad weather was here to stay, and most important, that *Bagan* had been under tremendous strain for the past 135 days and she was being run by a crew that would run out of its recently restored reserves in a matter of hours.

We slipped away from the city docks in Ketchikan on that 29th day of October and found our weather immediately. Despite the NOAA forecast, winds filled in from the southeast peaking at about thirty knots and drove a relentless and freezing rain sideways, slashing against *Bagan*. We were now heading down Alaska's famous "Inside Passage"—an area whose cruising season is short and one that we had missed by weeks. No longer would we have to worry about powering through the night because there were plenty of anchorages to be found along the way. But our hands were full with the infamous tides in that part of the world. It wasn't unusual to experience currents that could race through narrows up to ten knots.

If your timing was right, you could follow a favorable tide that would add many miles to a shortened day. At one point, we had all sixty tons of

Bagan scooting over the bottom at a very respectable fifteen knots. However, if your timing was wrong, you'd get jammed and lose equally as many miles holed up in an anchorage waiting for the moon to do its twice-daily magic. The timing of the various cuts and passages was something that challenged my exhausted brain to no end. Having Sefton running the boat was perfect timing for me and a great load off my shoulders. His grasp and wonderful ability with numbers got us to just about every narrow pass to take advantage of the powerful currents.

The Inside Passage is a circuitous route from the south of Alaska into British Columbia. From there, it is a direct shot down and into Seattle. At slightly more than 1,000 nautical miles, it threads through some of the area's most beautiful inland cruising grounds rimmed by snow-capped mountains and glaciers. Wildlife is abundant and fellow travelers and cruisers are always a radio call away—during summer, that is.

We were now well into the off-season, heading into winter. These were now waters whipped and pounded by storms that produce winds in excess of forty knots for days on end. Put these forty knots of wind up against a very adverse and powerful countercurrent and this area can produce some of the world's worst and most dangerous conditions. Again we found ourselves in the position of not being able to stop for any extended length of time and wait out one of these systems as a two-day wait could very easily turn into a two-week wait.

And here's where my one act of conscious disingenuous behavior came into play. Each morning before Sefton would awaken and come up to the pilothouse to prepare *Bagan* for the day's run, I would have already been up and listening to NOAA's weather broadcast for an hour. If he was getting up at 5:30, I made sure to get up to the radio in the pilothouse by 4:30. Very quietly I'd listen to what the weather systems were doing on and off shore, listen to the wind and sea predictions, and decide whether to put my own spin on these forecasts. My spin consisted of lies; if NOAA called for "excess of thirty-five knots" I'd report it to the crew as "excess of twenty-five knots." If the seas were to be a maximum of six to eight feet, my spin would lower them to four to six. Whether I was fooling anyone, I'll never know. My aim was to try and keep the threat of the ensuing nasty weather to a minimum. I did have my limits though. If I heard any forecast of winds over forty-five knots, we would stay put for the day. My goal was to eke out as many miles as possible each day and at least make a small dent in our progress to Seattle.

As we worked our way south in the passage, we did have our days of sitting on the anchor in some tucked-away anchorage, waiting for the passing of the latest full gale, listening as the rain pounded on the deck overhead and the waves crashed against the rock shore just outside of our protected cove. We'd sit tight and watch as wind-driven spume would fly up and over us as we waited for a break in the current gale.

The proverbial "cabin fever" was long-gone. To suffer from this ailment of tedium, one has to have a modicum of drive and energy, something we were all lacking.

Even the tease of Seattle being only a few more days down the line couldn't raise the needed strength to have the feeling of needing to leave—now.

We worked our way south to Petersburg, Alaska. In 1994, I'd brought my Nordhavn 46 *Gryphon* up from Los Angeles where I'd been living on her at the time, and cruised the passage, ending just north of Petersburg. As we currently made our way past this community and down a long, snaking channel called "Christmas Tree Lane," I noted to myself that I had completed my full circumnavigation of North America. If I had had a bit more energy, I would have celebrated, but I couldn't muster the energy to rise to the occasion.

Curiously though, I did find I had something left inside. When we made our turn down into "Christmas Tree Lane," we had a bus-sized slab of ice loom out of the ever-present fog and stand between us and the entrance. *Bagan* was easily maneuvered around it but I have to say that the whole time it was in sight, I was in a disturbing flashback to our time in the ice. My heart began to race, my palms began to sweat, and my spirits dipped dramatically. I wasn't calm until a few hours later.

The Queen Charlotte Islands in British Columbia marked one of our last open dangers because here the protected Inside Passage opens up to the Pacific Ocean. Storm-driven seas can keep this area in a state of violent and unforgiving conditions. Hundreds of ships have succumbed to storms of inconceivable destruction as they tried to make their way past this island grouping either inside or outside. Trying to protect ourselves from a guaranteed slamming, Sefton plotted a course well east of these islands down into Finlayson Channel where we were hoping to take advantage of a small anchorage, aptly named "Bottleneck," that the pilot books called "bomb proof." But not before the computer crashed, yet again.

When it finally came back up, we'd lost all but the electronic navigation program and with that, all our routing. This constant crashing was something we'd become used to by this time and had found and perfected many "workaround" solutions. There was a reason we all had Macs and not Windows.

Perhaps 500 yards in circumference and found at the end of a very narrow, twenty-yard wide, quarter-mile–deep cut, "Bottleneck" anchorage was walled in by steep, rock-rimmed cliffs on all sides. It was a steady thirty-feet deep all the way up to the water's edge. No beaches or gently sloping rock formations but sheer cliffs that vertically dropped down directly into the anchorage. With winds and driving rain in excess of fifty knots, Mother Nature ranted and roared outside in the channel not a quarter-mile away. We were snug, secure, and well-anchored inside, and after a full crock-pot dinner of beef stew and potatoes, all climbed into their bunks to wait out the gale, which according to NOAA, wouldn't last more than a few days. Whether cruising the Caribbean or crossing an ocean, if you spend enough time on a boat, your senses sharpen and perceptions become more acute. On an anchor or underway, lying still in a bunk you can sense the slightest of wind shifts or even feel that the boat has changed the direction it was pointing when you fell asleep. All senses become alive and responsive, especially your "sixth sense." I knew that something was deadly wrong the next morning at 4 a.m., when I was jolted awake from a deep sleep. It wasn't a matter of lying still and gathering my thoughts. I knew it was far too late for that. I jumped into my sweats and flew up to the pilothouse. The noise of rain being violently driven into the sides of *Bagan* was as apparent as the feeling of her bow being pitched up and down. A quick look at the wind gauge showed a sustained forty-three knots with gusts more than fifty knots. It was pitch-black outside and with a blanket of rain covering us, there was zero visibility. The compass was dancing about madly as was the wind point on the wind gauge. Every few seconds, I could feel and hear a deep rumble, a short burst of throbbing after which *Bagan* would seem to jerk spasmodically. By now, Dominique was awake and beside me with Chauncey and Sefton scrambling up from below.

No one said a thing. We had all risen from our bunks with deadly concern. What probably took mere seconds seemed like minutes. Chauncey looked up at the wind gauge and said "Holy shit" as he saw the numbers flash up and over fifty. Sefton slid open one of the pilothouse doors and the cabin was blasted with what seemed like nothing short of hurricane-strength wind, sharp, stinging rain, and the wild spume of tortured waves. He wasn't long in shutting the door. Again, another deep, quick rumble and shudder of reaction.

Bagan then slammed as she had done in the monstrous seas we'd been dealing with for the past month. It made no sense. We were in the most secure of anchorages that was all but sealed off from large seas. Another slam. And once more a sharp and deep rumble told me that we were dragging our anchor—with a rock-faced shoreline not twenty feet behind us. Somehow the demonic winds outside had found us. We were being buffeted by seas large enough to lift and drop all sixty tons of our boat. For waves to grow substantial enough to have this power, they need an uninterrupted "fetch" of at least several thousand yards to build up in height.

We had been no more than fifty yards from any of the sheer granite walls that the winds were now pushing *Bagan* down onto at a great rate of speed. As the deep rumblings told us, the anchor was no longer holding, and despite the zero visibility in the blackness of the gale-filled night, I knew contact with the jagged and strong rocks to be imminent. All I had to say was, "We've got to get out of here and now." Everyone fell into the respective roles they've been performing for the past 8,000 miles. I made sure Sefton didn't mind my jumping in over his command (he didn't) and started *Bagan*. Even though the radars and GPS were all active and working, the half-second lag that each one gave was a deadly half-second. Equally, I couldn't rely on the lag in the compass to show us our way out. We couldn't see a thing. *Bagan* could be facing west and the radar would show the distant exit as north. I'd turn her to the north, and by the time the radar showed north, the powerful wind would have pushed us well past our mark and we'd now be facing east.

Checking the instruments, the wind-driven over-correction would take no longer than two seconds. But in that short amount of time, we would go from facing the exit shown on the radar to seeing with our spotlight a steep granite-faced wall no more than ten feet away being pummeled by four-foot wind-driven waves. From the foredeck, Chauncey would call out: "Rocks, back her down!" I'd gently push her in reverse then pour on the coals. Dominique from the stern would then holler: "STOP!! Rocks ...!" I'd take a look at the radar, try to anticipate its next swing, put *Bagan* in forward, crank the wheel all the way to port or starboard, and give her a large shot of power to try to swing her stern away from the rocks. Before he'd get a chance to say it, I'd see the rocks lit up by the rain-slashed beam from the searchlight in Chauncey's hand. "STOP ... rocks!" Back and forth we went, each maneuver taking perhaps three seconds. We were driving blind and at any moment a broadside blast of gale force wind would push all fifty-seven feet of *Bagan* violently sideways, something I could only tell by the new way in which she was leaning and taking the confused seas.

By this point, our collective goal was to keep *Bagan* moving. Getting out was beside the point. With visibility impossible, this futile maneuvering was all done by feel and it was only when we were seconds away from certain destruction on the rocks that I'd know the outcome of the attempt. We were in a very small and prison-like washtub of confused and large seas driven by winds that were cascading down the sheer-faced mountains—winds that came from all directions on the compass at once. The scenario was the same one that we faced a month earlier as we left the Aleutians into the Gulf of Alaska. But there we had room to maneuver, time to try and figure out the beating we were taking. Here we had none.

"Back down, back down, back down... Ledge!" Sefton's searchlight had seen what Chauncey's didn't as we were quickly being pushed down and onto a twenty-foot ledge not three-feet deep. I quickly tried to remember the state of the tide. If we were to be pushed onto the ledge, I'd need to know how long we'd potentially be hung up on it before we were smashed to pieces. I put her in reverse, cranked the wheel to the right, fired up the thruster, and leaned on both throttle and thruster toggle, but the thruster appeared to be dead.

Bagan was slammed by a wave on the starboard side that was so large its water blocked out one of the ports on that side's door. How in God's name could such a large wave be generated in such a tiny pocket of water? She was again pushed down toward the ledge and this time Sefton didn't have to alert me. Again in reverse, I tried to move her away from the sharp underwater protrusion. We were holding our own but in each maneuver were losing ground. Imagine being in a ten by ten-foot, pitch-black room with a blindfold on. You seemed to remember that the door you came in through the previous day was ahead of you. Or was it? As you try to slowly make your way towards the door, people are pushing you, others telling you to not go any farther forward because you're about to hit a wall, then someone pushes you from behind toward that wall. You pause for the briefest of seconds to get your bearings when no sooner than you stop, someone pushes you from the side, then from in front of you. This chaos continues until your original plan to find the door changes to simply not hitting a wall.

Dropping the anchor was futile. In the few seconds it would take to hit bottom and bite, we would have been pushed up and onto the rocks.

Sefton hollered out, "We've a bit of open water ahead. If we go halfway across..." *Bagan* bumped. She bumped again. An invisible hand gently pushed her stern to port as she bumped yet again. My heart was in my throat because

I knew what this meant but refused to believe—that the five-month, 8,000-mile trip was going to end this way. I put her in forward and applied the throttle. Nothing but engine noise. She bumped another time and shifted further to port. In the darkness, I felt a slight lean to the same direction. I progressively and with great determination increased the throttle until her RPMs were at 1,500—cruising range. Nothing. In case her forward motion was so subtle in the maelstrom around us that I missed it, I looked at the GPS to see if there was any indication of movement. Nothing. I opened up her throttle all the way, this time maxing out the RPMs. She shifted to port farther and settled. Nothing. Soaking wet and still in his sweats, Sefton came in from outside and through the pilothouse. As I asked him to get me some water to drink, I all but choked on my words. Apart from the hollering of commands, no one had spoken during the past fifteen minutes—and as I now did so, I found my tongue and mouth bone dry, almost powder. I couldn't speak for the intensity of the fear and confusion.

Sefton's eyes were wide open and as wild as the night around us. I mimed that I'd like the water that he had brought up from the galley. "Are we screwed?" he asked. "Dunno," was as comforting a response as I could manage. I took a sip of the water and the cool liquid felt as though it was cutting my dry and rough tongue. Sefton went back out onto the foredeck and as he did I suggested that he get some lines ready. I think my words were lost in the gale because there was no response from him as he slipped back into the black, wet night. Twenty minutes into this nightmare and I had no idea where we were in the tiny anchorage, I vaguely knew which direction we were heading, and as things seemed now *Bagan*'s stern was hung up on some rocks. I'd no idea if it was a shelf or a single pointed pinnacle of a rock that would pierce her hull. Slowly I lifted the microphone to the foredeck hailer to call Chauncey and Sefton back in to tell them we needed lines out, life vests, ditch kits, and the dingy, which needed to be prepared. For the briefest of seconds, I allowed myself to feel that it was over, all of it.

Yet reflex found me grabbing the throttle one more time and I laid into it. With unexpected great power, *Bagan* lurched ahead and blasted a wall of water out onto the rocks behind her as she powered away from where we'd just been hung up not one second earlier. At the same time, I could hear Chauncey call from the foredeck "I think I can see the opening!" something that the radar hadn't yet locked into. From behind me, Dominique told me to keep my course. The electronic charts finally had a few seconds to lock in and translate the GPS reading onto the monitor and from what they and the two radars were now showing us, we were heading for the tiniest of cuts not forty yards away. Waves from the sound outside were funneling down through this small, twenty-yard–wide cut and *Bagan* was being tossed dangerously close to each steep-sided rock wall on either side. The sky was beginning to brighten and in silhouette I could see our way clear out into what seemed to be a hurricane-churned Finlayson Channel ahead of us.

"Holy shit. That was so much worse than the ice. Jesus Christ."

Dominique was standing beside me as we entered the five-mile–wide channel and headed south. "We almost lost her didn't we?" Not for the first time in the past five months, I was simply beyond words.

"Yeah, I thought we had." I responded. "Thought that we'd come all this way to sink her 200 miles from Seattle." Had she gone down in there, the walls were so steep that no radio call would have gotten out. So steep that there was no place for us to wash up on. In my mind's eye, I watched as all four of us were slammed, time and again, onto the rocks with a force and fury beyond anything survivable.

It was blowing in excess of fifty knots in the channel, but it was open. The wind was behind us and the tide was going south. While the ride was anything but comfortable, at least we weren't fighting it. NOAA weather said that the front would intensify but would start to fall apart that evening. We just needed to hang on and hope. From time to time that day I saw from great elevations, micro-bursts of air slammed down onto the water, flattening the sharp, steep seas and violently shooting the surface water off 100 feet in all directions, a remarkable and sobering sight. One hit the boat and it sounded to all of us as though a boulder had fallen on us. So powerful was the concussion that Chauncey ran up to the boat deck to make sure all was intact.

As the storm raged into the day, we continued to work our way south, passing between small islands that would give us a momentary respite before we rounded them, only to get thrashed again by the wind and waves. Sefton drew us some courses that kept us in the lee of the weather long enough for it to start to run its course and fall apart. Tired and exhausted, a theme we'd all shared for the past four months, we took refuge in small anchorages as we made our way south through Queen Charlotte Strait, Johnstone Strait, down into the Straits of Georgia and on to Seattle.

Two days outside of Seattle, we were once again forced to find a small anchorage to hide out from yet another building gale. NOAA's weather broadcasts for the area called for full gales for the next three days. We were automatons by now, reacting only to situations that were more than extreme and life-threatening. Between Chauncey, Dominique, Sefton, and me, there wasn't a voice or thought that felt we should wait until the wind dropped to a reasonable twenty-five knots. But our thinking was more along the lines of, "If it's not hurricane force, we should try it." By this time, we were four individuals, emotionless and exhausted, and were simply sleepwalking, laboriously putting one foot in front of the other to simply get a few more miles down the road.

With the promise of nothing under forty knots until we reached Seattle, I did an engine check one morning and found a bilge full of hydraulic fluid. The thruster had long since given up the ghost, so I wasn't sure why this fluid appeared so suddenly. It didn't take long for me to see that a hose in the stabilizer locker had ruptured, rendering them useless. We had 150 more miles to go with the promise of continued gale force winds and no stabilizers. We were limping in, but as fate or God or luck would have it, any seas we took were on the bow, not the beam. We didn't need the useless stabilizers. At 7:30 at night, on November 5 and in a full gale, *Bagan* and her small crew of four finished what they had set out to do five months and 8,500 miles earlier. In the driving rain, the crew landed and secured *Bagan* to the docks of Seattle's Elliot Bay Marina. Four exhausted and drained bodies continued to fight the elements as we headed *Bagan* into her slip and shut down her magnificent engine for the final time. Don Kohlman of Nordhavn Yachts stood on the dock in that stormy evening and caught the dock lines as the four of us maneuvered *Bagan* into her final position. Apart from Don, there was no great fanfare, no celebration, no arrival party, no crowds.

As we were tying her up and comically trying to get our land legs, Sefton summed it up.

"We made it."

We had made it. We had done what very few truly felt we would be able to do. Despite huge and at times horrific odds, we had made it. We made it from the Atlantic to the Pacific oceans through one of maritime history's greatest challenges, a route through the brutal Arctic that over the years had claimed hundreds of lives, quickly and quietly snuffing out them and their efforts.

Yet, far more important, we made it in a more powerful sense. Chauncey Tanton, Dominique Tanton, Sefton Theobald, and I made it back into each other's lives, uncovered and rekindled a family connection and love which, as so many of these things go, could have remained buried for many years into the future. We were now indeed a family by every sense of the word and if the past five months were to enrich my life, they would do so by simply this fact alone.

It was a few weeks later that we all learned something that we had no concept of five months earlier; that together, as a new united family, the four of us saw that *Bagan* became the first production powerboat in history to take on and complete the Arctic Grail, the Northwest Passage.

CHAPTER 18

REFLECTIONS

It has been more than 18 months since we shut down *Bagan*'s engine that rainy and windy night in Seattle. Lots of time to recuperate and reflect on what my family and crew did during the summer of 2009. I write this from the safe and secure vantage point of a small island in Maine, the very one where I learned to sail so many years ago. My desk sits before a picture window looking out to the east to Monhegan Island. During the course of this writing, some days have been sunny and beautiful, others gray and stormy. So much has our trip to and through the Northwest Passage become a part of me that on stormy, gray days my stomach tightens and my body remembers those five months. The trip to and through the Northwest Passage has forever changed my life in ways I least expected.

Yet I wasn't the only one aboard that summer, nor were my experiences and feelings the only ones altered. Equally as important, if not more in their own ways, are the reflections and thoughts of my three wonderful and brave children, each of whom I've asked to contribute feelings and thoughts about those amazing five months we shared.

So, below, in order of birth, are their words:

CHAUNCEY:

Since returning to the real world, I've been working on my MBA and other various entrepreneurial ventures in Denver. In my spare time, I have taken up refurbishing motorcycles, finished remodeling my home, and am currently restoring a fourteen-foot runabout.

As for the trip itself: My biggest worry was about the potential tearing apart of what family bonds were already in place. At one point, I had said I would rather not go at all if it meant that irreparable damage could arise. I guess we knew the stakes and it seemed all-important to maintain a constant respect, patience, and understanding for all that were on board, traits not inherent in my temperament. Going into the trip, my relationship with Sefton was strong but sensitive. Dominique and I had a troubled past, filled with poor communication. I had barely spoken to Sprague in years. I had never really met Greg. And Clinton—my sister's boyfriend for years—and I had only spent a couple of weekends together. For purposes of our trip, everyone in my eyes was equally family. Success pertained more to our collective ability to maintain even tempers and not so much the reliability of *Bagan*, the weather, or the waves.

I was amazed and surprised at how calm and respectful we all were. We had a few brief and laughable flareups, but overall it was a remarkably drama-free voyage considering how serious and consequential the Northwest Passage is. There simply wasn't any room for it. Throwing a temper tantrum wouldn't change anything, and given the gravity, duration, and seriousness of our voyage, mature attitudes were all-important. Most surprising was the ease at which we joined together. I had entirely underestimated the time we had spent together growing up. As it turned out, we were all very used to spending time together under one roof.

Most powerfully were the bonds that grew out of facing real danger, handling it professionally, and rejoicing thoroughly. I think we all understood that each of us was reliable. My bonds with my family, the earth, animal kingdom, and the seas have never been stronger or deeper. My spirit flies free in the barren deserts of the high Canadian Arctic and when I pass, my last thoughts will undoubtedly rest in the vast, peaceful, and harsh landscapes we experienced as a family.

DOMINIQUE:

I returned home and am now working on my BS in nursing. I still dream of life at sea and hope to do more traveling, though maybe with a bit less ice.

It has been a year and a half since we left the dock and started heading north on a journey to complete the Northwest Passage. From the start, that's just what it was, but almost as quickly as we let the lines go, this journey became much more.

I have done a lot of traveling, a lot of boat deliveries. Spent many hours contemplating life, my purpose, my future, and my past. Before I left on this trip, I thought I knew the value of life and family, friends and love. At its end, I realized I have much to learn.

Directly after the trip, I took a few months of solo time in Seattle—a chance to regroup and reintroduce myself to life. I was hired by Sprague to look after *Bagan* and make sure she was still sound, still strong. I did much the same for myself. After three months in Seattle, I was ready to head back to the East Coast, to Newport, the place I've called home yet never let my feet anchor. I was ready to anchor.

This was easier said than done. I came to realize that for the past six years, I have been a floater, a vagabond, a free spirit. My mind changed as quickly as my location. Never fully committed to anyone or anything. Ready to bolt when things got too constricting and expectations too high. I was hiding from myself and from others. That was what I needed to change to become the person I dreamed of being.

I needed money, and boats were all I knew. I came back and did freelance work that at least allowed me to be home every night and sleep in my own bed. I had a hard time embracing my life like I once did. My perspective had changed. Since completing the Northwest Passage, I found that I wanted more from life. I wanted a secure and stable future. When the boating season was ending and most of the boats were heading south, I enrolled in school to pursue a degree in nursing. This was something I had started years ago but the timing wasn't right and now I know it is.

Since last January, I have been a full-time student taking classes at the local community college, concentrating on my prerequisite work for a bachelor in nursing. The trip to and through the Northwest Passage taught me more about myself and my family than I thought I'd ever know.

SEFTON:

Since I've returned to normal life back home in Denver, I have been finishing college and becoming a part of the local music scene. To this day, I'm influenced by the power of the trip. Even while snowboarding, I can't help but see the strange world I was once accustomed to. The trip was my first major travel venture, and the Northwest Passage has sparked my desire to travel and explore as much as possible of this world.

Aside from myself, a packed suitcase, and a room full of nerves and anxiety, my house was empty before starting the trip. That night before I caught a flight to Halifax to meet up with the rest of the crew was the last night in the society I was familiar with. It was the last night in the known world. It was the last night before the Northwest Passage.

A month or so had passed since I hopped aboard and we had finally made it to Greenland. This was the point that truly marked the trip as a journey. Somewhere in between dodging icebergs and exploring fjords, I had reached the feeling that this was an adventure incomparable to anything else. I was eager for more. I couldn't get enough, and with every step I took, I gained more perspective on how Arctic cultures exist, which in return provided perspective for my own world I left behind.

As weeks passed, we finally entered The Passage itself. To me, this entrance symbolizes the second chapter of the expedition. No longer did we see massive icebergs or brightly painted Greenlandic buildings. This was an area extremely bare and desolate. Though the wildlife was plentiful, including walruses and polar bears, it seemed we had stepped into a realm that all had forgotten or have yet to discover. The landscape was minimal with geological patterns everywhere. This was such a surreal part of the trip. I remember coming top deck and wondering if this was just some crazy dream. It had been a couple of months from any real interaction with the normal world and our normal selves and it would still be months until that normality returned.

As we exited The Passage, we were reacquainted with beautiful scenery. No longer was it only pebble beaches that rolled on, almost resembling Mars. Instead we saw huge, snow-covered mountains and lush flora along the southern Alaskan coast. This was the area that I saw as the third and final leg of the trip. With the monstrous waves of the Gulf of Alaska behind us, this was the calm walk to the finish line. There was so much beauty here, although we were unable to fully appreciate it since after five months at sea, we were all pretty ready to get back to our lives, back to the real world.

I feel that each leg of the trip provided something different. The first was raw adventure and excitement. The middle leg showed just how bizarre this world can get when you are almost the farthest away from society one can be. The final leg was actually the hardest for me, almost a test of my sanity. Though broken into different segments, a constant theme of family was ever-growing throughout the entire trip. Although I had already known my family members well, new sides of people and new dynamics were always arising. Even if you think you know someone well, there is still a wealth of information to be learned while spending five months on a boat with each other.

With this further understanding of my siblings and father, I was happy to see the strengthening of family bonds that resulted from this adventure. This will be something Chauncey, Dominique, Dad, and I will have forever, not only the memories of the trip but the deep and growing bonds of family, something as precious as the environment we saw.

Though this trip was unique and life-altering, the feeling of finally coming home was priceless. I had stepped back into Colorado as a new person with a new attitude. I guess this was because I am now one of the few in the world who can say they completed the Northwest Passage.

SPRAGUE:

I knew that I was going to be coming back with mental as well as physical images of sights few have had the opportunity to observe before, just as I knew that five months aboard a fifty-seven–foot trawler would leave me with experiences that up until this point I'd only known in controlled doses. That lives and communications would be pushed and tested to all previous limits was a given. What I didn't begin to consider before we left was what lay beyond those limits. For the basic pressures and liabilities of mounting such an expedition as well as ensuring that it keeps moving ahead day after day, mile after mile in a positive and constructive flow were at times overwhelming, relentless, and unforgiving. Add to this the extreme weather that had to be met and dealt with, not ignored nor hidden from.

If my years have taught me anything, it is that if we're always honest and open with ourselves about our fears and negative experiences, we always bounce back from adversity and will enjoy wonderful and positive experiences all the more. Those very same positive experiences made, for me, the trip a brilliant success from which I brought back untold treasures. But only upon closer examination and in those moments of deep reflection I found that not only did I bring back something, I left something up in the Arctic as well.

Neither of these were anything tangible nor the expected "lessons learned," for they reached far deeper and if allowed, into a far more emotionally charged area than that. What I left up there was innocence and the feeling that with enough preparation, foresight, and belief that for the most part things will "always work out."

While this belief usually works in the everyday world, we were far from that world. Reflecting on our time in the ice and the horrific weather we had to endure, I find my belief in that one innocent thought, that "all will work out," was yanked from me and upon closer examination failed to pass scrutiny.

The extremes we faced had no use for optimistic sayings. I strongly feel that because we were at times given the chance to see yet another day, it came from guidance and grace, some would call it luck, from somewhere off the boat.

It is interesting when looking back at the trip, to look at those who didn't feel there were powers at play far greater than us, for they sadly didn't last the journey. They fell tragically, not being able to honor their commitment to themselves or the rest of the crew.

Nothing in life is a given. And never was it more true than up there where, if Mother Nature and her fates decide it so, lives can be snuffed out in the blink of an eye. At times, our fates and the fate of *Bagan* were entirely out of our hands and it was the grace and kindness of Mother Nature's elements that allowed us passage; grace and kindness which clearly, in my mind at least, saw us on our way while saying, "Don't even think about coming back this way again!"

This was a warning which not for a million dollars would I begin to consider challenging.

There's also been a very unexpected sea change in my life: my relationship with the ocean. So many were the times on the trip that we pressed our luck, asked, even begged the unthinkable from both boat and Mother Nature that I feel that were I a cat I would have used up ten of my nine lives.

I tapped into my vat of sailor's luck and am now running a bold deficit. I have always had a larger-than-life respect for the sea and what she manages to hand us as we work our way across her; sometimes we're in her favor, others not. During this trip, I felt a total indifference from her that led me to know and experience simple raw fear, no frills, no adrenalin, no wild rides. In the final analysis it boiled down to black or white, success or failure, life or death. I overstayed my welcome and both she and I know it. It's because of this feeling that I know my credit and goodwill with the ocean are decisively over. I'll forever stand in awe of her majestic power and the remarkable role she played in my life, and the joy, adventure, and beauty that she shared with me.

But as in all meaningful relationships that run their course, you know when the time comes to say good-bye. Suffice it to say we love each other dearly but have a need to see other people. I will miss her.

Yet it wasn't all fear and narrow escapes. For as I continue to write these words, I know that I, we, all came back with a taste and respect for some indescribable power which surrounds and protects us in dire times. Ever since I got clean and sober thirty-three years ago, I have felt we weren't alone in our daily existence. Call it predetermination or a collective unconscious, there is something besides us at work around us. Nowhere did we feel this more than at Beechy Island. Simply put, we were not alone. A few days later, when we made it up to Griffin Inlet, we had the same feeling. But here we also felt we were not wanted. Many times our experiences were tested beyond all previous levels of comfort.

When we were stuck in the ice and simply had no options left but to exist, something bailed us out.

Just as when we were sure *Bagan* was going down in the small anchorage "Bottleneck," something altered the experience enough to allow our escape.

Since our return, people have been asking me all manner of questions about the trip. (My favorite being, "Did you ever have to consider cannibalism?")

There have also been questions about global warming and the potential for shipping through The Passage. During the trip, I tried to ask those we came in contact with those same questions and much to my surprise, found that up there, as with down here, the answers were as varied as complex.

I'm not an expert on the environment. I don't work in the field nor do I study the environment. Apart from the research that I did for the trip, the people I spoke with, and what I personally saw, my observations about global warming are my own and have very little hard, cold science to stand behind them.

While filming for the intended documentary, Chauncey and I interviewed two groups of people: Inuit elders or those younger that worked in fields associated with the environment. In each case, these interviews took place in Cambridge Bay, a fairly large community that also serves as a transportation hub for the Nunavut Territory in northern Canada.

Almost to the person, the younger people said winters were getting shorter and easier while the elders said they felt the winters to be getting longer and harder. One of the younger Inuit, who worked for the Department of Fish and Game, felt that the winters were coming on earlier and lasting longer into spring. There, just as down here, was no set consensus and diverse observations were as easy to find as conflicting statistics.

Yet there was one thing that they all did agree on, that there is indeed a change. Whether it's the condition of the ice—"slush" being a new concept to some elders—or the appearance of old ice where new ice once existed, there is a change going on and to what degree of severity depends on with whom you talk.

After coming away from meeting with various people along the route, I also felt thoughts and conclusions about global warming came down to localities. Due to flukes of nature, one community could experience a less severe winter than another 100 miles down the road. This difference could greatly influence one's perception of what or wasn't happening on a global basis.

One of the main objectives for the trip and documentary was to come away with a fairly precise understanding as to the state of environmental affairs. I'm sorry to say that in this I failed. But I have an excuse. The heft of Mother Nature's intentions was introduced to us far sooner and to a much larger degree than ever anticipated and became a very large part of our daily lives. By the time we got to The Passage, the scope and aim of the trip was simply to finish in one piece. The time planned for interviews and casual observations had turned into a race against the seasonal clock and we had to be satisfied with the few interviews that we got. Quickly the story of the trip changed focus from overview and observation to not getting hampered by the elements.

To have missed some planned interviews and time spent among the various communities in exchange for surviving the ordeal was fine with me. There's a saying that in the 1800s, those hearty souls who took a stagecoach journey across the United States started off with great excitement and anticipation of all that they would see and encounter. By the end, they were just happy to reach their destinations alive. Never was it as true as with our trip to and through the Northwest Passage that summer.

The second area I wanted to investigate and learn from was the potential of commercial shipping through The Passage. What I learned from those I interviewed was more focused and defined compared to their beliefs on global warming. While some small commercial shipping does currently exist and some more will certainly start up, all of whom I spoke with felt that the large-scale supertanker-type of shipping would never happen.

I was told that when the area is frozen, perhaps more than three-quarters of the year, it provides not only migratory routes but ice roads as well. To one extent or another, all of the communities from the smallest fishing camps to larger ones like Cambridge Bay depend on these ice roads in and out of their area. Any interest in larger commercial shipping would meet great resistance.

The Northwest Passage is, for the most part, an uncharted area. When we were able to take soundings in some locations, the bottom would be ten-feet deep, then drop to perhaps a hundred feet, then come back up again to ten feet, all in the stretch of perhaps a quarter-mile.

It's my feeling—as well as that of many of those who live in the Nunavut Territories—that if commercial concerns want to use this shortcut between the two major oceans, there would have to be extensive surveying and dredging to accommodate their needs, perhaps negating some of the immediate profits to be found. In dealing with the ice, shipping will find it to be completely unpredictable and each year it would present its own grave challenges.

Without the promises of immediate profits, I don't see these concerns to have a large concentration span. Again, these are just my thoughts based on observations by the few who live up there and are by no means steeped in feasibility studies and corporate research.

One area that doesn't seem to grab the headlines as much as global warming or potential shipping, but to me holds a far more frightening potential for disaster, is that of the natural resources to be found in and around The Passage.

The exploration of lucrative natural resources just under the surface is something that I feel could destroy one of the most delicate and pristine ecosystems on our planet. There are five Arctic powers vying for dominance: Russia, Canada, Denmark, Norway, and the United States. Unlike Antarctica, there is very little paperwork in place delineating which nation has what claim to which area. Far too complex to try to break down in this writing, suffice it to say it's a bit like the Old West, all trying to stake a claim via interpreting antiquated laws and rulings to their benefit.

What's at stake is something that could completely and utterly destroy the region and everything north and south of it faster than any effect of global warming; the rabid and unmonitored search for natural resources. When it comes to trying to find and remove oil and gas deposits while keeping the area intact, man's track record stinks.

Profit trumps protection and excavating through the area's fragile permafrost layers could be a disaster waiting to happen. It has been estimated that the Arctic holds one-quarter of the world's remaining oil deposits—almost twice as much as Saudi Arabia's reserves. If for any reason the hunt and removal of the oil and gas were taken off the table, the area also boasts a phenomenal amount of materials such as lead, magnesium, zinc, nickel, and diamonds. The largest fear I have about potential excavating is the "out of sight, out of mind" concept.

To back up this fear are events not widely known; that between 1958 and 1992, Russia deposited 18 nuclear reactors in and around the Arctic Ocean, several of them still loaded with nuclear fuel. Few, if any, have been located and retrieved or cleaned up.

As with Chauncey, Dominique, and Sefton, my reintroduction to the life I left on June 16, 2009, has been a rich if not at times curious one. Very little of it has been as expected. The three kids and I are in touch much more frequently than we used to be and enjoy a bond and love which, in my wildest of wishes, I never felt possible. I feel blessed beyond description in that not only do I know these three people but that they are family and we all share this remarkable experience and a growing love for each other.

I have received an email suggesting I dishonored the memory of those courageous explorers who went before us in that I did the transit on a "money sled" and insulated myself from the true history of The Passage. Ironically, the author of this email didn't have the courage to sign his name.

Many times there have been misunderstandings about the financial side of the trip and several people both close to the trip and some not associated with it, have been laboring under the misconception that because there was a brief media interest in our accomplishment, the checks and cash have come pouring in. How I only wish that were true.

And quite a few posts on nautical blogs claimed that I was reckless and cavalier with the lives of my family and crew and that I was the type that, if stuck, would be the first to cry for help regardless of putting the lives of those who'd come to my aid in peril. It was hard to see how these folks could come to such a conclusion without ever meeting or talking with any of us.

Yet not all of the discomforts related to the trip have come from the outside. From time to time, many of the fears I discovered along the way still play havoc with my thinking but far from the extent they did during our times of desperation. The black line I saw still exists but doesn't carry the same threat it did when we were stuck in the ice or getting pounded relentlessly on the final third of the trip. The hard times allowed me to recognize this barrier and to this day it still lurks. But it is far from the threat it was then, apart from a few exceptions.

Gone are the daily pressures of mounting such a project: liability and the responsibility of my children's lives being the most demanding. I still have the occasional nightmare of being trapped and sinking and, when looking out onto storm-tossed waters will, at times, find me coming up short.

My personal experiences were pushed and broadened so much that the adventure has expanded the boundaries I feel in everyday life. Because of the trip, I feel I am now aware of much more about our daily existence and what it has to offer, both pro and con. While the daunting aspect of the black line exists, the flip side is that I can readily see all the positives in my life in much more vibrant colors. Possibilities are endless and potential unlimited. The transit to and through The Passage has allowed me to see and take in most everything around me with a greater and deeper appreciation; such as the wonderful people who showed us daily support; people who followed the trip on the site, read about it, or simply learned secondhand of our attempt to transit The Passage.

Hundreds of congratulatory emails have been printed out and sit in a folder on my desk reminding me daily of how blessed and lucky we were to have participated in such a journey.

Since the trip ended, some memories have become a bit less clear, while others simply need refreshing. Most every time I get together with various crew members, there's usually a chorus of, "I forgot all about that!" Yet one memory, a feeling I know will never need refreshing, is the feeling of being "allowed" into such hallowed and historic grounds, the haunting threat of isolation which bears down on each of the few who have transited The Passage. This overwhelming feeling of drama and tragedy staggered even the least sensitive of us. Being brutally aware that for seemingly hundreds of miles in any direction, empty horizons lay, brutally stacked up, one after the other for as far as the eye can see. I will never forget the overwhelming feeling of how frail and pitiful mankind can be when he's in an area he has no cause to be in.

That, plus the very basic lesson that were we to have to defend ourselves against the hidden, storm-driven forces of nature, the only and easily defeated defense that we possessed would be our arrogance and ignorance.

Yet we were allowed through. The five months we were underway gave us memories, sights, and feelings that no encounter I can conjure ever could.

I am humbled and blessed and forever I'll carry with me the blessings that were heaped upon me, upon us, during our transit of the Northwest Passage that summer of 2009.